# THE DRIFT INTO DECEPTION

## The Eight Characteristics of Abusive Christianity

# THE DRIFT INTO DECEPTION

*The Eight
Characteristics of
Abusive Christianity*

## Agnes C. Lawless
## with John W. Lawless

kregel
RESOURCES

Grand Rapids, MI 49501

*The Drift into Deception: The Eight Characteristics of Abusive Christianity* by Agnes C. Lawless with John W. Lawless

Copyright © 1995 by Agnes C. Lawless and John W. Lawless

Published in 1995 by Kregel Resources, an imprint of Kregel Publications, P. O. Box 2607, Grand Rapids, MI 49501. Kregel Resources provides timely and relevant resources for Christian life and service. Your comments and suggestions are valued.

Scripture quotations, unless otherwise noted, are from *The Holy Bible: The New International Version* copyright © 1978 by the International Bible Society. Used by permission of Zondervan Bible Publishers

Cover & book design: Alan G. Hartman

**Library of Congress Cataloging-in-Publication Data**
Lawless, Agnes C.
    The drift into deception: the eight characteristics of abusive Christianity / Agnes C. Lawless with John W. Lawless.
        p.  cm.
    Includes bibliographical references.
    1. Heresies, Christian—United States—Controversial literature. 2. Cults—United States—Controversial literature. 3. Discipling (Christianity)—Controversial literature. 4. Lawless, Agnes C. 5. Lawless, John W. I. Lawless, John W. II. Title.
BT1476.L38        1995        273'.9—dc20            95-8342
                                                                            CIP

ISBN 0-8254-3163-8 (paperback)

1 2 3 4 5 Printing / Year 99 98 97 96 95

*Printed in the United States of America*

To Ken for his patience

To Linda Medill Hall for
her encouragement and belief
in this project

To our critique-group members
who have helped fine-tune this book

# Contents

# Introduction

**It Can't Happen to Us!**
April 19, 1993. The eyes of the world watched the terrifying spectacle on their television screens. As though spewed from the mouth of a fiery dragon, thick, black smoke and orange flames devoured the wooden fortress.

Inside this inferno, leader David Koresh, some sixty-seven adults, and seventeen children perished. The Branch Davidians' Day of Armageddon arrived on the plains of Waco, Texas.

Amazingly, Koresh started out in a mainline Seventh-Day Adventist Church before joining this splinter group in 1981. Together they drifted into outright heresy.

But, you say, that can't happen to us. We're too smart.

That's what we thought.

We both accepted Christ as our Savior when we were children. Reared in Christian homes, we attended evangelical churches. We graduated from well-known Bible colleges and universities. We did graduate work. We had devotions every day, for we knew the importance of Bible reading and prayer. After marrying we even spent seven years overseas with Wycliffe Bible Translators.

Surely we would never drift into deception.

But we did.

But, you ask, doesn't one have to be in a *cult* to be deceived? Deception is not a problem in evangelical, Bible-believing churches, is it? And what in the world is an "aberrant" Christian group?

But in all good faith, we got caught in one and drifted with the rest of its members towards the shoals of deception.

How could that happen? As you read, we hope you too will learn that aberrant Christian groups are a growing menace, that they use cult-like methods to draw and control adherents.

### All Are Lost

Imagine a crowd climbing aboard a sight-seeing steamer for a cruise on Lake Erie and around Grand Island on the Niagara River in upper New York State. It's a beautiful day with sunny skies. People throng the decks to play games, to watch the scenery, or to doze on lounge chairs. A small band plays romantic melodies. The ship enters the river past the city of Buffalo and the eastern side of Grand Island. But instead of turning south at the northern tip, the steamer continues on towards Niagara Falls.

The captain tries to turn the ship around. Nothing happens. The wheel is useless. The rudder must be malfunctioning. He shouts instructions to his crew to cut back the power. The steamer slows. Now it's drifting. The helpless captain and crew are frantic. But they mustn't let the passengers know the seriousness of the situation . . . not yet.

Soon a small boat pulls alongside. A person on deck shouts through a megaphone toward the wheelhouse, "Danger ahead! Turn around! You're drifting towards Niagara Falls!"

Passengers line the rails. What's happening? they ask one another. Is something wrong? Surely not. The man in the little boat must be crazy.

The captain comes on deck. "Don't worry!" he shouts. "Everything's okay! No need to panic."

The crowd settles back on their deck chairs. The band plays on.

Caught in the rushing flow of the river, the steamer picks up speed as it drifts toward the falls.

Faster. And faster.

Over it goes through the spraying water. Down it plunges 190 feet into the boiling cauldron and is broken to pieces on the rocks below.

Today we Christians are just as blind to impending danger. Hoping for exciting spiritual experiences, we join the crowd climbing aboard the "cruise ships" of evangelical "superstars." As the band plays, we sing rousing choruses. We listen breathlessly as famous leaders, dressed in designer suits, promise us health, wealth, and self-fulfillment. All for a price, of course.

Occasionally a small boat pulls alongside. A person with a megaphone yells, "Danger ahead! Turn around!"

But our leaders come on deck. "Don't listen to him!" they say. "He's crazy! Nothing's wrong."

And then we hear the roar. We see rising spray from the falls of destruction. Only then do we realize that our ship is doctrinally rudderless. We're drifting toward the Niagara of deception.

And the band plays on.

Because of our experience, we learned that we can all drift into deception if we loosen our moorings and ignore the winds of false doctrines. In this book, we want to show you how vulnerable we all are. The names of individuals who have shared their stories with us, however, have been changed to protect their privacy.

The prologue which follows tells our personal story in allegory form, perhaps better than we could tell it otherwise.

# Prologue

### A Parable

"Help, Lord!" I yelled into the darkness. A strong wind blew pelting rain against me as I struggled down a rough path in the forest. I was a middle-aged sheep, along with my special ram. We were trying hard to follow our undershepherd.

But sudden panic gripped me. Was he going the right way? Something seemed terribly wrong.

"Good Shepherd!" I called. "Please show us what to do."

I thought back to a beautiful spring day in the valley where we sheep wintered. I lay in a lush meadow listening to the laughing of a nearby brook and a delicate melody from my Shepherd's flute. I stretched my full length on the green carpet and let the golden rays of the midday sun warm my body. Ah, life is good, I thought.

I noticed the undershepherds gathered around the Good Shepherd. While they rested under a shade tree, he taught them from his Book of Instructions. He told them how to love and care for the sheep under his direction.

The lazy spring days passed slowly. I grew fat on rich grass and clear water. As the weather warmed, the Good Shepherd and his helpers prepared for the difficult trek to summer meadows in the mountains. We would move higher where the grass was lush, the water clear, the air cool. A hot summer in the valley would parch fields and dry streams.

Soon all was ready. The shepherds carried supplies on their backs and staves in their hands. Deftly, they organized us into a compact flock and began the journey with the Good Shepherd leading the way.

I moved into line next to my special ram and followed along. One of the undershepherds walked beside us. Adept at telling jokes, he kept us entertained as we traveled. Sometimes we laughed so hard we could scarcely keep our hooves on the trail.

Day by day our flock climbed higher into the mountains. At first the path was wide and smooth, but gradually it narrowed to little more than a track. We became exhausted from climbing, so we gladly bedded down each night in a grassy area our Shepherd found.

The terrain grew more wild as we moved higher. The Good Shepherd often looked back to see how we fared. He shouted encouraging words and sent his undershepherds to help those of us who stumbled or fell.

One evening a storm blew up before we reached shelter. Black clouds scudded across the sky. A bitter wind whipped through the mountain pass. A cold rain slanted down in blinding sheets, making the path a slippery quagmire. The undershepherds slogged through mud to check on us, giving a pat of encouragement here and a pull there. They told us that the Good Shepherd was pushing on to a protected pasture. We were to keep close together and to follow him up the trail.

My friend and I stumbled along the slippery path as best we could. We often found it difficult to keep up with the sheep ahead of us.

Suddenly out of the rolling mist and rain, the undershepherd stepped into our path. We hardly recognized him with a hooded raincoat over his shepherd's garb.

"Hello," he said. "Say, I have something to tell you."

"What?"

"The Good Shepherd is taking you over a dangerous route." He spoke in a loud voice to include the other sheep around us. "Why, it's a wonder you haven't all fallen off the cliff in this storm long ago!"

"Is there a better way?"

"Sure there is. I know a shortcut that's much easier than the old straight-and-narrow path you've been climbing. In fact," he added with a broad grin, "most of the flock has gone on without you now, so you'd better follow me. We'll soon catch up with the others."

With a gasp, I realized that most of the flock had indeed climbed on. My friend and I and a number of others had been left in the rain and darkness while we listened to this man.

Hesitantly I looked at the ram beside me. "What do you think we should do?" I asked softly.

"Well, maybe he can show us how to catch up to our Good Shepherd. If he knows a shortcut, it's worth a chance."

"But is it safe to take another path?" I asked. "What if we get lost?"

"I'm sure it's okay. This undershepherd acts as if he knows where he's going. Anyway, he's doing us a favor."

"Come on, gang. Let's go!" the man shouted. He scrambled up the hillside like a mountain goat. We left the muddy trail and followed him, slipping and sliding. Soon we reached a wide, smooth path.

When we stopped for breath, the shepherd sidled up beside us. "I'm glad you've made the right choice," he said with a grin. "You'll never regret it. I'll take good care of you."

I smiled back. He does seem nice, I thought. He has a wonderful personality. With his wide smile, he's almost handsome.

As we gathered around him, the shepherd said, "If you have any questions on our hike, ask me. Don't bother thinking for yourselves. Just follow me!" He patted his expansive chest.

As the new shepherd led the way, my ram and I trotted along with renewed vigor.

"Since so many of our friends have come along, we can't all be wrong," I said. "Doesn't that give you a safe feeling?"

My friend nodded.

After climbing awhile, we came to a plateau. The storm had abated, and a full moon rose over the mountain peak, bathing trees and meadow in a shimmering glow.

The shepherd looked at us sympathetically. "You poor lambs have had a rugged climb. You must be exhausted! But before we bed down for the night, let's have a little fun. The Good Shepherd wants us to be happy, you know."

He pulled a flute from his pocket and played a merry tune. As the lilting notes filled the air, the shepherd beat time with his foot, then began dancing.

We sheep slowly followed, forming a large circle around him. Joining front hooves, we danced on our back ones, swaying in rhythm. As the ethereal music played on, we lifted our heads to the sky. All weariness vanished. An exquisite joy flooded our beings. We felt we could stay in this moon-bathed meadow forever.

When the music stopped, we clamored around our new shepherd.

"That was wonderful!" enthused a young ewe.

"I've never experienced anything so thrilling," I told him.

The shepherd smiled broadly. Raising his hands, he motioned us to be quiet. "You're all beautiful sheep, and I love you. Now, why don't we all move over to those trees and rest? I want to talk to you."

We skipped to the grove of shadowy trees with our leader. "Before we go to sleep," he said, "let me tell you how honored I am to have you follow me. A shepherd couldn't have a finer flock than you. I'm at your service. I want to help you all I can. Now let's get some rest."

As we lay down on the soft grass, the shepherd gave each one a hug and a pat on the head.

I snuggled closely to my friend. "Isn't he wonderful?" I asked. "He's so kind and loving. He really cares about us, doesn't he?"

"He seems to." The ram yawned, stretched, and was soon fast asleep.

However I lay awake at first, thinking about all that had taken place that day. I still was doubtful about following this shepherd instead of the Good Shepherd. But our new leader was so nice, so jolly, so sure of himself. Anyway we'd soon catch up to the others. It must be all right.

The next day dawned clear and sunny. After we grazed in the meadow and drank from a sparkling stream, the shepherd gathered us around him.

"Listen, sheep, we have some rough going ahead. You'll need more care than I'll be able to give you, so I've asked three of the rams to help out. Come up here, fellows."

When the big rams ambled toward him, the shepherd counted us off by threes. He told the "ones" to go with one ram, the "twos" with another, and the "threes" with the last.

We slowly sorted ourselves out, then stood quietly by our leaders.

"Good for you!" the shepherd said. "If you have any questions or problems, go to your leader. Then he'll check with me, okay? Follow him carefully and give him the honor and loyalty he deserves. Get to know the other sheep in your group, and build committed relationships with one another. That's what will hold us together in tough times."

The shepherd pulled a small book out of his pocket and read a few lines from the Good Shepherd's Book of Instructions. He closed it and said with a smile, "That's a wonderful book, but I don't think we should have our noses in it all the time. We should live the right kind of lives and not just fill up on head-knowledge. If you follow me and your leaders, you'll get along fine. Trust us. Okay, let's go. Remember to stay in your groups."

With that, the shepherd started off across the meadow, then took a path through the woods. We trotted along behind, singing lively choruses and chatting among ourselves. The ram leaders were kind to all and helpful to those who needed encouragement.

"Are you enjoying this?" my friend asked me.

"I love it! I've always wanted this kind of personalized help and direction. Now we're going places. We should catch up with the rest of the flock in no time."

Day followed day as we moved through the woods and fields. When we stopped to rest and graze, the shepherd taught us more about his philosophy of submission to authority.

"Sheep, this is the 'now word' for today!" he often said with vigor. "Let's not be content with our old ideas. Let's press on to be the best flock around."

The way to achieve that, he said, was for us to submit to the ones over us. We ewes were to submit to our rams, the rams to one of the three leaders, and the leaders to the shepherd.

It all seemed so organized.

One evening when the flock rested, the shepherd said, "You know, as sheep your nature is to go your own way, to do your own thing. But if you do, you'll soon be lost in the woods or eaten by wild animals. We can't have any rebellion in the group."

We shivered at the prospect.

He went on, "You used to simply follow the Good

Shepherd and his Book of Instructions. But now I have a better way to reach the high meadows more quickly and safely. Tonight I want you to submit to your leaders. That way we'll become a tightly knit group that can really forge ahead."

The shepherd asked his three leaders to move out across the grass and their groups of sheep to surround them.

Then on signal, we sheep bowed our knees in submission. We each took turns saying, "I honor you as my leader and promise to obey you."

Finally the head rams bowed before the shepherd and promised him loyalty and obedience all the days of their lives. Under the shimmering moonlight, the ceremony was solemn.

The shepherd then spread his arms wide and blessed us.

As time went on, we moved through the mountain forests and meadows. We flourished under the kind, loving care of our leaders.

However, as the weather worsened and the path grew rough, tempers frayed. Once when I slowed down from weariness, my leader nipped me in the rear. "Get a move on, will ya?" he growled. "We're supposed to keep together as a body, and you're holding us up." I tried not to cry and moved closer to my friend.

To save time, the shepherd dispensed with our midday rest and kept us traveling. One day we were almost overcome with weariness as we stumbled along the rough trail.

When the leaders reported to the shepherd that we were uncooperative, he turned on us impatiently. He pulled a whip out of his long sleeve and cracked it over our heads. "Hurry up!" he shouted. "We've got a lot of ground to cover before nightfall."

Startled by our shepherd's change of attitude, we scurried along, panting and puffing.

Our shepherd drove us mercilessly all that day. The sun went down behind the mountain peaks, so he led us to a dark cave. We flopped on the ground, too tired to graze. As he played a soft melody on his flute, we dropped off into sound sleep.

During the night I dreamed that the shepherd carefully cut off my fleece, then did the same to all the flock. I suddenly felt chilly, snuggled closer to my friend, and slept on.

When a gray dawn broke through the mist, I awoke with a start. I looked down at myself in the dim light. So it wasn't just a dream after all! That man had fleeced me—and the rest of the sheep too. Without moving, I watched as the shepherd hid large bags of wool behind boulders deep within the cave.

As the sun came up and the rest of the sheep awoke, they were astonished to find themselves bare. One ram, bolder than the rest, trotted over to the shepherd and asked, "What happened to our fleece?"

The shepherd stared back at him.

"*You* took it, didn't you?" the ram accused. "What right do you have to cut off our wool? It belongs to the Good Shepherd!"

"Shut up, you dumb sheep. I've been taking care of you, haven't I? So naturally the wool is mine." Holding his rod across his chest, he glowered at the rest of us. "Any more questions?"

We all shook our heads fearfully.

"Okay, grab some breakfast and let's be off."

We filed out into an open area in front of the cave. Since the grass was sparce and brown, we shoved and nipped each other to get the best clumps. We were weak and hungry, for we had had nothing to eat the night before.

After the leader rams rounded up our little flock, the shepherd led us down the trail through the woods.

I trotted beside my friend quietly for a while. Finally I whispered, "Do you get the impression that we're gradually going downhill?"

"I've wondered that myself."

"Do you think this way really is a shortcut to the Good Shepherd's upper meadows?"

"I just don't know. All we can do now is to follow the shepherd. If we strike out on our own, we'll get lost."

On and on we walked with no time to rest and graze, even at noonday. Tired and hungry, we stumbled along, our leaders yelling to keep us in line.

By late afternoon dark clouds moved across the sky. Since the path now led through a deep forest, we had trouble seeing our way.

I shivered as a sharp wind blew upon my bare skin. My misery was accentuated when cold rain pelted me. Once I tripped over a sharp rock and fell. "Help!" I cried.

The shepherd strode over and yanked me to my feet with his hooked staff. "What's the matter with you anyway?" he snarled. "Can't you keep up with the group?"

As I limped over to my friend, the shepherd hit me with his rod. "Take care to stay in line," he growled.

I nuzzled up to my friend and stumbled along beside him. "Something is terribly wrong," I whispered, "and I'm not sure what. This shepherd is so different from our Good Shepherd. When he gives us pep talks, he sounds wonderful, but at times he seems cruel. Do you think we should stay with him?"

"Of course. I'm sorry about what happened to you, but I don't see anything really wrong. Our friends are going along with it, so it must be okay."

I wasn't convinced. I had heard the undershepherd's snarls and felt his blow on my back. Oh dear, I said to myself, what shall we do? We can't find our own way in the dark. But there's something about that man I don't like.

Suddenly, I remembered that our Good Shepherd had often told us, "Call unto me, and I will answer you." So I prayed, "Dear True Shepherd, please show us what to do. If you want us to continue following this shepherd, then give me peace. But if you want us out of this situation, then deliver us!"

By this time, I noticed that the path led along the side of the mountain. On our left rose a sheer wall of granite. On our right dropped a gravel bank, covered with bushes entwined with vines. Since the trail slanted downwards, the shepherd was leading our flock at a swift pace, in spite of the darkness.

Suddenly, I heard a voice call my name.

I stopped. "Yes, what is it? Here I am!"

I listened, but I could hear no sound, only the moaning of the wind and the splash of the rain.

My friend turned around. "What's the matter with you?"

"Oh, nothing, I guess. I thought I heard someone call my name, and I knew it wasn't your voice. I must have been mistaken." I walked slowly along with the ram.

Then I heard it again.

This time the voice was urgent. As I skidded to a stop, I fell over a large rock.

My friend came over to investigate. "Are you all right?"

"No, I've hurt my leg."

As I struggled to get up, I put out my good front leg. I felt nothing but empty air. Backing up, I cautiously sniffed around the area.

"Get back!"

"What's the matter?"

"We're on the edge of a cliff! The path has given way in the storm. One more step, and we'll be over."

Trembling, we crept as far away from the precipice as possible and huddled against the granite wall behind us.

Rubbing my injured leg, I prayed, "Thank you, dear Shepherd, for calling me. Forgive us for wandering off your path. We'll follow only you from now on. Just help us out of here."

Then we saw the Good Shepherd striding down the path towards us out of the misty darkness.

After carefully binding my leg, he picked us both up in his big arms and climbed up the trail. Soon we were back on the straight-and-narrow path leading to his upper pastures.

As we approached the main flock resting on a meadow, I whispered in my Shepherd's ear, "I won't ever leave you again."

I could see his smile in the growing light.

"Yes, my child," he said as he hugged me closer. "And I'm sure your lame leg will remind you."

# Part I:
# Drifting with the Current

# Chapter 1

# Caught in the Drift

To reach the port of heaven,
we must sail sometimes with the wind
and sometimes against it—but we must sail,
and not drift, nor lie at anchor.
                    —Oliver Wendell Holmes

*Agnes*

One summer when I was a teenager, I attended a summer camp at Gull Lake, Alberta, Canada. My friends and I spent our afternoons perfecting our diving skills from a raft some distance from shore.

One day three of us were so busy swimming and diving we didn't notice that the other campers had left the beach. We paid no attention to the dark clouds growing on the horizon. Even though the sun was still warm, a wind blew up, ruffling the water.

"Do you have the feeling that we're drifting?" one girl asked, standing on the raft and shading her eyes. "We're past the camp."

One of our number was Eleanor Beckett, our French and Latin teacher in high school. She pulled on the anchor chain, which relaxed in her hands. "It's come off!" she shouted.

By this time, we realized the wind, now sharp, was pushing us down the long lake and farther from shore. Black clouds quickly covered the sky, blotting out the sun. Heavy drops of rain puddled the water.

Eleanor, a strong swimmer, said, "I'll go for help. You girls stay right here." She dove over the side and swam to the beach.

We watched her run toward the camp, then disappear up the path. We sat down on the raft and prayed, shivering in the cold, heavy rain.

Soon we saw Eleanor running back down the beach. She strode through the shallow water, then swam towards us, her strong strokes slicing the waves. Suddenly, she stopped and waved one hand weakly in the air.

"She's going down!" I shouted and dove in.

My friend followed, and we swam toward her. We turned her on her back, pulled her along, and dragged her onto the raft.

As we lay exhausted on the wet boards, our cold skin dimpled with goose bumps, we watched two staff men pushing a boat into the water and rowing towards us.

Soon we were back at camp—warm, dry, and thankful to be alive. We vowed to always check our anchor chain and the signs in the sky.

## Hungry for Something More

After we had spent seven years in the Philippines with Wycliffe, Agnes had major surgery. Lengthy physical complications made it necessary for us to return to the States and to resign from the mission. Getting back to normal took several years.

While Agnes was still recuperating and in need of encouragement, we heard of a lively, growing church. It wasn't too far from our suburban home, so we visited it on a Sunday morning in February 1973. We walked into the foyer where the tall, good-looking senior pastor greeted us with a big smile and warm words of welcome.

We entered the crowded sanctuary and found seats near the back. The congregation was made up of nicely dressed middle-class people. Unlike the conservative churches we had been used to, young and old clapped and sang Scripture choruses enthusiastically. A piano, electric organ, and a small orchestra, complete with drums, hammered out the beat. A large choir helped lead the singing.

As we listened to the pastor preach, our hearts were touched. He gave a well-organized, simple message that fed our hungry spirits. No wonder this church is crowded, we told each other afterwards.

We began attending regularly. The Sunday-evening services were as packed as the morning ones. People from other churches added to the crowds. The pastors and prominent guest speakers preached dynamically and convincingly. We felt privileged to sit under their ministry.

Even the services on Thursday nights were full of rousing singing, testimonies, and excellent expository Bible studies. The pastor handed out well-organized outlines of his lessons. Again we felt fed with solid spiritual food.

As time passed, the church was so crowded that the board decided to build a large multipurpose building. It served as a gymnasium for their elementary school as well as an auditorium for Sunday services. With two balconies, it easily seated two thousand. The church planned to also use it for citywide rallies with special speakers. Once the new structure was up, it was filled morning and evening on Sundays.

Before long, we joined a home Bible-study group. The friendly host and hostess did much to encourage us all, especially singles and young people with problems. Occasional potluck suppers increased the feeling of closeness in the group.

After one meeting, our home leader approached John. "I've been asked to be an elder in the church. Since that will take up much of my spare time, would you be willing to take over the home group?"

John hesitated. "Isn't there someone else?" he asked. "Leading a meeting isn't exactly my gift."

"We can't think of anyone who could do a better job. And you live close by."

"Well, I'll pray about it with Agnes and let you know."

A few days later, John told the elder that he would take the position until someone more suitable came along.

So we met Tuesday nights in our home. How we loved to sing! Beginning with lively praise songs, we sang chorus after chorus, then moved into quieter worship numbers. Our hearts were prepared for John to give a brief Bible study, usually something he gleaned from his own quiet times with God.

Following that, John asked for requests, and we had a time of prayer. If someone had a special need, we gathered around his chair, laid hands on him, and prayed for him. The evenings closed with refreshments and sharing. A feeling of love enveloped us all. We felt close to the Lord and to one another.

As our friendships developed, we showed our caring in tangible ways. Greg and Jackie suffered financially when Greg was laid off work. With several children, they were hard pressed to keep food on the table. The group brought groceries to tide them over for several weeks until he found another job, and we contributed money for his wife's eye glasses.

On another occasion, the men helped a young couple move into their new home. The women served a potluck dinner afterwards. We felt like one big family.

### The "Florida Five"

As time went on, speakers from Florida occasionally came to our church for special services. The "Florida Five" were well-known in national and worldwide charismatic circles for their dynamic personalities, humor, and solid Bible studies. Their teaching eventually became known as the "discipleship/shepherding movement" and then simply the "shepherding movement."

Soon our pastors went to nationwide rallies and conferences conducted by these men. One summer thousands jammed into a large coliseum in the Midwest to hear them.

In a sincere effort to help new converts, the Florida men decided that these "sheep" needed shepherding. So they trained leaders to take this responsibility.

Eventually the Fort Lauderdale men taught that every "sheep" needs a shepherd. Each sheep should submit to his shepherd so that he could receive the best possible care and teaching. When one teacher was at our church for special meetings, our senior pastor announced that he had "submitted" himself to this man.

"Every pastor needs a pastor too," he said, "and I've found mine."

Our tall minister went over to the short one and put his arm around his shoulders. They looked like the proverbial "Mutt and Jeff" with beaming faces.

From then on, things changed in our church.

## "New" Revelation

After our pastor submitted himself to the leader in charge of the West Coast, he regularly flew to California for leadership meetings. Each time he returned, he was flushed with the excitement of being close to one of the "Florida Five"—his favorite one at that.

"People," he preached, in effect, "we need to be open to what God is saying. This is the 'now word' for today! Let's not reject it or be content with our old beliefs. Let's press on into this new truth and go all the way for God!"

One way to accomplish this, Pastor told us, was to listen to tapes and study books put out by the Florida leaders. He also encouraged us to subscribe to their monthly magazine.

More and more, although we were unaware of it at the time, our pastor based his preaching on the teachings of these men. He implied that this "new" truth was not available to outsiders and that it was a restoration of pure biblical Christianity.

On the other hand, we noticed he gave little or no teaching on the importance of personal, daily devotional times with God by reading the Bible and praying. He didn't come right out and say that private study was unimportant, but he repeatedly made slighting remarks about people who "keep their noses in their Bibles all the time, but don't live it out."

"Don't fill your minds with 'mere head-knowledge,'" Pastor said. "Too many Christians worship the Bible. That's 'bibliolatry.' God has something fresh to say to us today."

One Sunday as we drove home from church, I said, "I'm baffled by Pastor's remarks about 'bibliolatry.' He doesn't mean we should give up Bible reading, does he?"

"No, of course not," John answered.

"But what about young converts? What if they *think* he means they don't need to read their Bibles or pray?"

Sure enough, we found this to be true. One evening in our home group, John spoke about the importance of daily devotions, then asked the people to share their methods. We were amazed to find that few read their Bibles regularly. Apparently most relied on "predigested meals" from the pulpit.

This implied teaching became even more clear one evening during a potluck dinner with other home-group leaders. The elder in charge emphasized the need for close relationships with our people. Then he asked all of us to tell what we most desired to see happen in our home meetings.

When it came our turn, John said, "We'd like our people to learn to have a daily quiet time with the Lord."

"Yes," I added, "we all know that the most important aspect of our spiritual lives is a vertical relationship with God. Out of that will come good horizontal relationships with one another."

To our surprise, the elder looked seriously at us and said, "I disagree with you. Our first responsibility is to develop meaningful horizontal relationships. Out of these will come our relationships with God."

We were too astonished to reply. None of the other home leaders said a word.

## Authority and Submission

Just what was this "new" truth, this "now word for today" our pastor and the Florida teachers talked about?

The cornerstone of their teaching was authority and submission. They believed that God appointed leaders to exercise authority over believers in all matters of faith and practice. Their followers were to submit and obey.

They taught that independence in thought and action was equivalent to rebellion. Man's "great transgression" was rebellion—the unwillingness to submit to authority. The way to overcome this was to submit to those authorities and obey their commands.

## Pyramid Structure

To implement their teaching, the "Florida Five" set up an elaborate religious pyramid structure with themselves on top followed by area leaders [later called "bishops"], presiding elders [pastors], church elders, home-meeting leaders [later called "pastors"], and laymen, women, and children. At each level of the pyramid, people were expected to submit to and obey those over them, just as to the Lord himself. Such obedience included all matters of faith and practice.

When our pastor echoed the teachings of these national leaders that "every sheep needs a shepherd," he meant that each of us needed someone over him to lead him into a more mature Christian walk.

Christ the Good Shepherd, he said, "is the pattern of what every shepherd ought to be." Like Christ, he is

- to know the sheep
- to be known by the sheep
- to call them by name
- to lead them
- to provide proper pasture (spiritual food)
- to protect them against the thief and the robber (Satan)
- to lay down his life for the sheep

The sheep are

- to hear (recognize) the shepherd's voice
- to follow and obey him
- to honor him
- to submit to him

Pastor and these other leaders warned that if we did not follow our individual shepherds, the "wolves" would get us, that we would be subject to satanic attack. However, if we stayed under the "covering" and protection of our shepherds, we would be safe from spiritual danger.

Just who was our "shepherd"?
For the "five," he was God.
 For a bishop, he was one of the five.
  For a senior pastor, he was the bishop.
   For an assistant pastor, he was the senior pastor.
    For a church elder, he was an assistant pastor.
     For a home-meeting leader, he was a church elder.
      For a layman or a single woman, he was a home-meeting elder.
       For a married woman, he was her husband.

A shepherd, we were taught, was fully justified in giving strong advice to those under him in all matters of belief and practice. If a home leader saw one of his group having trouble with finances, he should correct his wrong methods. If family members were not getting along well together, he was to confront them and set them straight. If a home-meeting leader was not conducting his meetings in the accepted manner, the elder over him should correct him.

Each "sheep," on the other hand, was to submit to his shepherd, either vocally or in writing. If he had to make a major decision, such as buying or selling his house, changing jobs, or getting married, he should first consult his shepherd, then follow his advice.

Each sheep also was to honor his shepherd in every way possible. He could mow his leader's lawn, polish his car, give him gifts, or take him to a ball game. A woman disciple could clean her leader's home, take his wife out to lunch, bring his family food, send them flowers, or take care of their children.

Home meetings were emphasized in this teaching. There we made solid relationships with other disciples and formed strong commitments to one another. There too, leaders could "build into people's lives." By that they meant they could instruct them according to this teaching.

Fed to us in small but constant doses, we gradually assimilated this teaching. It seemed so right. Surely it was scriptural to "obey those over us in the Lord." Yes, we thought, of course we should submit to them and not be disobedient and rebellious.

With our pastor under the headship of the famous teacher, we felt we now had an "inside track" that would help us grow in our Christian lives as never before. Visions of spiritual glory danced in our heads.

We were excited—and yet a bit uneasy at the same time.

## Women—At the Bottom of the Heap

*Agnes*

When we first started attending this church, we went to a home meeting in our neighborhood. One evening, I went alone, since John was busy with schoolwork.

The young leader explained the chain of command (as shown above).

"You women," he said, "should get your spiritual teaching and guidance from your husbands, not on your own."

His words didn't sink in until I got home and told John about the evening.

"Does he really mean that I shouldn't have my own devotions, that I shouldn't read my Bible and pray by myself?" I asked.

"Sounds like it."

"I've never heard of such a thing!" I said. "I'd have to wait a long time for you to hand out what I need."

John grinned. "Right."

The next evening, I phoned our home-meeting leader. "Did I hear you correctly—that women are to get spiritual food and direction from their husbands, that they shouldn't go directly to God in prayer and in the Scriptures?"

"Well, that's part of the new teaching the Lord is giving his Church today. That doesn't mean you can never read your Bible. But you should get the bulk of your teaching and guidance from your husband. He'll explain what he gets from me, I from my elder, and on up the line."

After I hung up, John and I talked about this aspect of the "now word for today."

"Let's just forget it," John said. "We know from experience that it won't work."

So I continued reading and studying the Bible on my own, in addition to family devotions with our son Ken. When a problem came up or I needed to make a decision, I talked it over with John as usual. We studied Scripture to see if God had anything to say about it, prayed about it, and resolved it together. As the biblical head of the house, John was a considerate leader.

The teaching of women submitting to their husbands or leaders intensified. I listened to others telling what a relief it was to let their husbands make all the decisions—even minor ones. All they had to do was to submit and obey. Sounded good. And carefree.

As I gradually absorbed this teaching, I asked John's permission or direction about every detail of my life and work. If I forgot, I felt guilty.

I was trying to conform, oh, I was trying.

But John felt overwhelmed dealing with his own problems at school and with mine at home. Finally he said, "God's given you a good brain. Use it! Come to me with just the big things, and we'll talk them over."

One evening we were at our elder's spacious home with the other home-meeting leaders under his care and their wives. After a potluck dinner, the men gravitated to the living room around the crackling fire. We women stayed in the dining room.

As I scanned the faces of these women, most seemed to look alike. Not in their physical features, of course, but they suddenly appeared like a row of little gray mice—all submissive, all obedient, all conforming—with no identities of their own.

On the way home, I said, "Honey, don't let me get like that!" I said it with some vehemence.

"Like what?"

"I don't know for sure, but those women all look alike. Like their personalities are squished."

John chuckled and squeezed my hand. "I won't let yours get squished."

### Our Uneasiness Grows

One Saturday morning, John and I were eating breakfast. The sun streamed through the large windows and ruffled, white curtains. We watched the branches of our birch trees dip and sway in the gentle breeze of our front yard. We ate pancakes and sausage between sips of hot cocoa.

I put down my rose-chintz cup and looked at John. "Honey," I said, "I feel uncomfortable about church."

"You do? Why? You're the one that always says on Sunday mornings, 'Oh, boy! We get to go to church!'"

"I know. I can't quite put my finger on it, but I feel uneasy about the changes taking place. Something is wrong, and I don't know what."

"Aw, you women are always getting 'feelings' about things. I don't see anything *that* different."

"Okay. Maybe it's just my imagination . . . ."

"Right."

The next morning when we arrived at church, we greeted friends warmly and enjoyed the rousing music and enthusiastic message of our pastor. My fears were allayed, and I forgot my concerns.

As changes picked up momentum under the guidance of the national leaders, however, my uneasiness returned. The church structure became more pyramid-shaped. Pastor's anointed messages, which he had received from his own Bible study, became less frequent. In their place were "warmed-up leftovers" from the famous Florida Five. The emphasis was on submission to authority. On every sheep having a shepherd. On relationships with one another rather than with God. The Bible and a personal prayer life continued to be de-emphasized.

By this time, both of us were puzzled. What had happened? Surely this wonderful evangelical church that we loved so much couldn't be getting "off base"—or could it?

In my devotions one morning, I wrote a prayer which underlined my uneasiness:

If this thing is of you, Lord,
Quiet the churning of my mind.
Bring peace to my troubled soul.
I choose your way, oh, Lord.
But if this is not of you,
If the disquiet in my spirit
Is put there by you to check me
From following the teachings of men
Blindly,
Then I accept this uneasiness
As an indication that something
Is not right
And I should beware.
Make me so sensitive to your voice
That I will instantly hear
Your soft call
And follow you alone.

Weeks later, we received a package from John's mother. It was a book about "Shiloh," the commune in Maine where she was born and where her parents spent five years at the turn of the century. Entitled *The Almighty and Us*, it was written by Arnold White who had gone to Shiloh as a child with his family and grew up there.

While John spent most evenings correcting papers for his fourth-grade students, I read the book first. Later, I told him about what I had read.

"You know," I said one night, "things in that book sound strangely familiar."

"Like what?"

"The authoritarian structure the leader, Frank Sandford, set up. The way he controlled his followers reminds me of our church."

"Interesting."

Before long, John read the book, too. We agreed that, although Sandford's group went far beyond our church in off-base beliefs and practices, the similarities made us uncomfortable.

We decided to keep our eyes and ears open. Had we been caught in a drift?

## Questions

1. Describe the beginnings of the shepherding movement.
2. Why are people open to "new revelation"?
3. Which should come first—our relationship with God or our relationship with people? Why?
4. What is the cornerstone of shepherding teaching?
5. What is man's "great transgression" according to shepherding teachers?
6. Describe a pyramid structure.
7. What is meant by a "covering"?

# Chapter 2

# Breaking Free

Enlighten the people generally,
and tyranny and oppressions of body and mind
will vanish like evil spirits at the dawn of day.
—Thomas Jefferson

As we read the book about Shiloh that John's mother had sent, we felt uneasy. Some of its practices sounded strangely familiar. Was our church headed in the same direction?

One Saturday morning, we decided to make it a subject of prayer. "Lord, you know our quandary," we prayed. "We choose *your* will. Please show us beyond a shadow of a doubt whether we should leave or stay."

Within a short time, the Lord brought about circumstances that made our decision clear.

## Another Jonestown?

*Agnes*

It was a Sunday morning in Seattle, Washington, in November, 1978. As our green station wagon pulled into our church parking lot, my heart almost stopped beating.

"John, look!" I said to my husband.

"At what?" he asked.

"There—on the church wall!"

My eyes focused on black words roughly spray-painted across the white wall of our church: "Beware! Another Jonestown!"

Wide-eyed, I looked at John. My hands clutched my purse and Bible.

"Good grief," was all John said as he wheeled the station wagon into a parking space and stopped.

"What can that possibly mean?" I asked.

"Oh, I don't know. Probably some 'kook' who's left the church and is mad about something. Don't let it bother you."

After leaving Kenny, our ten-year-old son, at his Sunday-school room, we walked to the multipurpose building for our adult class. We entered the refreshment line, picked up Styrofoam cups of steaming coffee, and went to our class.

Sitting on folding chairs, we sipped our drinks and nudged a couple from our home group in front of us. Jim and Janet smiled broadly when they turned around and saw us.

"How're you doing?" Jim asked.

"Great! How about you folks?" John asked.

While the fellows talked about car repairs, I lowered my voice and asked Janet, "Did you see the writing on the wall outside?"

"Did we ever!" she said.

"What do you make of it?"

Janet shrugged her shoulders. "I haven't the foggiest idea. Maybe after hearing all the news about Jim Jones and Jonestown recently, someone got carried away. But it's stupid to liken our church to that awful mess." She nodded her short, brown curls.

"That's for sure," I agreed.

The two-hour service that followed Sunday school was crowded with some two thousand people filling the balconies and main floor. Nothing was said from the pulpit about the graffito on the outside of the church. By the next Sunday, the wall had been painted white again.

But those awful words—"Beware! Another Jonestown!" burned into my memory. I was to recall them only too soon.

### Another Warning

One Saturday morning, we drove down the freeway towards beautiful Lake Sammamish for our church's leadership retreat.

The scenery lifted our spirits—hillsides bristling with tall fir and alder trees, clouds like scoops of meringue floating across a blue sky. We left the freeway and drove along the narrow road that runs by the lake and the Bible campground.

Following others to the chapel under towering evergreens, we greeted friends. Inside the door, coffee urns puffed like little steam engines atop tables loaded with plates of sweet rolls.

We helped ourselves to refreshments, then took seats in the chapel. The unique room was shaped like a small amphitheater with wide, carpeted steps to sit on instead of chairs. At the bottom was a flat area with a fire crackling in a big, black stove. Through wide windows that stretched from floor to ceiling, we saw the sapphire-blue lake ringed with evergreens and backed by snow-crowned mountains.

The room filled with casually dressed members of the pastoral staff, elders, deacons, and home leaders. Accompanied by guitar, an assistant pastor led us in singing choruses.

Then our pastor spoke about *confrontation*. He said in effect: "Although I've talked about this before, I want to emphasize the fact that many Christians today have their lives in disarray. You probably have plenty in your own home group. If you see someone who needs to get his finances or his marriage in order, then you must confront him about it. This is your responsibility as a leader, but you need real courage to do it."

One young married man raised his hand, "I'm having trouble finding time to deal with people in my home group because of other commitments, such as choir."

Without a moment's hesitation, Pastor barked, "Then drop choir!" The forceful way he spoke and the hard look on his face jolted us. He seemed like a tough commanding general instead of the gentle shepherd we were used to.

After he finished speaking about confrontation, Pastor asked us to meet with our elders.

Eight of us gathered around our elder and his wife. "Let's discuss confrontation in more depth," our elder said. "What ways to confront do you like best?"

After two or three gave their opinions, John said, "Over the years, especially when we were on the mission field, we've found the best way to change people is to pray and let the Lord do it in his way and time. Confrontation is sometimes necessary, but too often it brings wounds which never heal."

The elder looked at him sharply, then went on to someone else.

After a tiring day with confrontation as the main theme, we were glad to get home.

*John*

A few days later, I met with my elder and other home leaders in our weekly meeting.

"I have sad news for you," the elder said. "One of our home-meeting leaders, Joe, committed suicide after the retreat."

We sat in stunned silence. A fellow finally said, "I noticed Joe that day. He really looked down."

"But why would he do a thing like that?" another asked.

"I wonder if the retreat was too 'heavy' for him," suggested another. "He may have felt he could never do all the things expected of him as a leader."

Later, when I told Agnes the news, she said, "Hmm, another warning."

## No Independent Yankees Wanted

*John*

Before long, pressure to conform was put on me as a home leader. I'm an independent Yankee from Maine, so I didn't feel the need to check with my elder about minor matters. In fact, my bimonthly private sessions with him became so uncomfortable that I dreaded them.

Although the elder was a kind man, he was confronting as he had been taught. "John, you really need to buy a new suit," the elder said one day. "Then circulate among the people on Sunday and *act* like a leader!"

One Saturday in June 1979, I watched Agnes spoon chocolate-chip dough onto a cookie sheet.

"Isn't it time for your meeting?" she asked.

"I guess so. I'm not too anxious. I feel like a little kid on his way to the principal."

"You're doing a fine job as a leader," Agnes said. "You're quiet and gentle, but our people appreciate your steady ways. We're having wonderful times as a group."

I had originally accepted the home-group leadership on a

temporary basis until someone else could be found. So we began praying about whether or not I should continue. I finally felt I could never be the leader the church wanted me to be. I could never confront our people and tell them what to do. Nor did Agnes feel like telling the women how to run their homes.

So I told our elder that we had prayed about the matter and felt that God wanted me to resign as home leader.

When our senior pastor heard about my resignation, he talked to us on the phone. He seemed upset.

"How do you feel about it?" he asked Agnes.

"Fine," she said. "We've discussed and prayed about it thoroughly. John feels this is God's leading, and I agree. Anyway, I don't have the time or energy to do all that a home-leader's wife is supposed to do."

"Why is that?"

"My health isn't too good, and I feel God wants me to do more writing."

"Do you mean to tell me that *you've* pulled John away from his work as home leader—just because *you* want to pursue your little 'writing ministry'?" The sarcasm in his voice was unmistakable.

We were both dumbfounded by his question, since her writing had not entered into my decision. I would have resigned anyway, writing or no writing.

As Pastor berated her, we were speechless. We couldn't seem to defend ourselves. His jumping to this conclusion with no basis, and his sharp, angry words stunned us both. When he finally said good-bye, Agnes burst into tears.

A few days earlier, she had been in his office about the writing she was doing for him. With a smile, he had said, "I just thank God for you!"

However, that evening of the phone conversation, we were having our last gathering of our home group under my leadership. Since it was a warm June evening, we had planned a potluck picnic in the park.

Agnes hurriedly dried her tears and finished putting together a creamy potato salad and a hamburger-rice hot dish. After packing our picnic basket with a red-checked tablecloth and utensils, we drove to our town park located on the edge of the lovely Sammamish River. We were almost the last ones there because of our delay.

Friends greeted us warmly as we set out the food. Several

looked at us quizzically, but said nothing about Agnes' red-rimmed eyes.

After we had eaten and played baseball, our elder and his wife joined us. We spread blankets on the grass to sit on, then sang choruses together. Finally the elder rose and told the group that I was stepping down as home leader. He kindly offered suggestions of other groups they could join, at least until he could appoint another leader. As we looked around at our dear friends, our hearts were full of love for them all. Parting would be difficult.

In his last session with me, our elder told me, "Pastor has gone through your giving records personally and feels you're not giving enough to the church."

"But we give a lot to our missionary friends. They need it desperately."

When I came home and told Agnes the gist of the conversation, she said, "That does it! You can go to that church if you want to, but I'm not. The nerve of him—going through our giving records."

Before this happened, we had no intention of leaving the church, and we planned to attend another home meeting. But now we felt we could never go back. Something had died within us. We decided to look for another church.

## The Trauma of Leaving

*Agnes*

Fortunately, summer had arrived, and school was out. We spent much of our time at our summer home on Bainbridge Island in beautiful Puget Sound, licking our wounds and attending my family's former church there.

One night I awoke suddenly. All that had happened in the past weeks rushed upon me. I sobbed over broken relationships with Pastor and our many church friends whom we loved so well. Depression settled over me like a gray quilt.

Later, when we were home again, I told a friend on the phone about the trauma I was experiencing. "It's as if I'm going through a divorce or the death of a loved one." My throat felt as if I had caught a fly ball with my mouth and had swallowed it.

"Why don't you talk to Walt?" she asked. "He's been through that too, you remember."

Walt had been a pastor and was now in a traveling ministry. He had served on the pastoral staff for several years at our former church.

After Walt left, Pastor told us in a leadership meeting that we were to have nothing to do with this man. To do so would mean disloyalty to him and to the church. Therefore, although we had often wondered what happened, we never had been in touch with Walt or his wife.

Now, however, I called him and explained our situation.

"Oh, I understand only too well," he said. "The same thing happened to me."

"It did? Can you talk about it?"

Walt explained that he had never taken a salary at church because he wanted to be free to accept speaking invitations from other churches in the Puget Sound area.

One day, Pastor asked him to come to his office with the other pastoral staff members. Pastor started off the meeting by emphasizing the importance of submitting themselves to him as senior pastor, just as he was doing to the national leader over him.

He looked at Walt. "You seem to be quite independent—doing your own thing. Are you willing to submit yourself to me for your direction from now on?"

"I've learned by hard experience not to submit myself to any man, but to submit to God for his leading in my life. I want to keep free to minister wherever I'm invited. Therefore, I would have to say no to your question."

"Why are you working with us, then?" Pastor asked.

"Because I love you all like brothers, and I rejoice to be a part of your ministry."

"But if you refuse to submit to me, you'll have to go!" Pastor said sternly.

The other men's faces were carved in granite. The issue was closed. Walt got up and quietly left the room—and the church.

After telling me his story, Walt prayed for us on the phone, then invited us to their home for an informal meeting.

The following Sunday evening, we drove to Walt and Anne's home in a suburb north of Seattle. Three other couples from our former church soon arrived. All of us had been wounded by our experiences there.

During the course of the evening, Walt explained from Scripture what was wrong with the shepherding movement. We appreciated the way he talked without rancor toward individuals. He had learned to forgive.

Walt further explained the necessity of breaking "ties" between our souls and those of our former leaders in order to get freedom from the bondage we had been in.

We took turns sitting in two chairs as couples while Walt prayed for us. He suggested we say, "I reject this teaching as heresy and refuse its influence in my life."

Then Walt laid hands on us and said, "In the name of Jesus Christ, we break the soul-ties between you and your former leaders."

From then on, my weeping stopped, my depression left, and the healing of my soul began. I could concentrate once again, and the Scriptures took on new life. Like the apostle Paul, "scales" seemed to drop from my spiritual eyes so I could see what the Lord had delivered us from.

### Down a Manhole

*John*

One Saturday noon, we sat at the kitchen table eating homemade vegetable soup and cornbread hot from the oven.

"You know," Agnes said, "we've never heard from any of our friends at church or in our home group since we left—and we've been gone several months now."

"True. I feel like we've fallen into a manhole, and they've dropped the lid on us."

"Exactly. I've called a couple of my closest friends and told them what happened," she added, "but I don't think they believed me. Might as well have saved my breath."

"Well, you remember what Pastor said about Walt when he left," I reminded her.

"And most of it wasn't true."

"I know, and he's probably said some exaggerated things about us, too. He can't have people think we left because we felt something was wrong with the church. So he puts the blame on us."

"Yes, and no doubt he's warned people not to have anything to do with us like he did when Walt left."

"Exactly."

## More Bleeding Sheep

*Agnes*

The shrill ring of the telephone broke my train of thought as I typed in my study. I picked up the receiver and said, "Hello."

"This is Bill," a young man said. "You don't know me, but I heard you used to go to our church. I just read the article you wrote called, 'Could Your Church Become a Cult?'"

"You did? Where did you get it?"

"Some of the young people at church made copies and passed them around. They sent one to us."

"Interesting. What did you think of it?"

"That's why I'm calling you. After reading it, I was so overwhelmed that someone understood what we're going through that I sat down and cried."

Bill explained that he had been raised in the Midwest where his father was a minister. He had heard our former pastor speak at his dad's church. Bill was so impressed with him that he moved to Seattle where he could sit under his ministry. He accepted everything the older man said and felt he grew spiritually under his guidance.

Before long, he met a young girl who had been raised in the church. They decided to marry and attended the necessary premarriage classes. This gave them further indoctrination into the shepherding teachings of the church as well as preparation for marriage.

"When we finished the classes," Bill went on, "we had a personal interview with Pastor. It all went well until near the end when his eyes seemed to bore right through us. He said, 'I'll marry you if you'll submit yourselves to me.'"

"Good grief," I muttered into the receiver.

"Something about the look in his eyes when he demanded submission to him scared us. We decided to get out of there—fast!"

"What happened then?"

"We left the office and the church and haven't been back. We still want to get married, but it's embarrassing to look for another pastor we don't know. He'd wonder why we didn't have our own minister marry us.

"Do you see now why I cried when I read your article?" Bill asked. "We had given that church and pastor our loyalty during those years. But now we're so upset," he added with quivering voice, "we don't care if we ever go to *any* church again."

I encouraged Bill as best I could before hanging up. As I fixed a cup of tea before returning to my typing, I prayed, "Lord, here are two more who have come out of that church wounded and bleeding. How long does this have to go on?"

## The Encounter
*John*

"Dad! Here comes Pastor!" Our thirteen-year-old son Kenny stared out the kitchen window as a sleek, black car pulled up in front of our house one evening in the fall of 1981.

I left the papers I was correcting and hurried into the kitchen. Kenny and I watched—horrified—as the car door swung open, and our tall former pastor emerged, then strode up our sidewalk.

"Oh, Lord, help!" I whispered as I answered the door. I didn't notice Kenny ducking under the long, yellow tablecloth on the dining-room table.

When I answered the door, Pastor marched in with a stern expression on his handsome face. The conversation went something like this:

"I've come to see you about this article you and Agnes wrote—'Could Your Church Become a Cult?'"

My knees shook, and my heart pounded. "Yes?"

"That certainly was a damaging article to me!"

"Oh? We didn't mention your name or the name of your church."

"You didn't need to! Everybody in the whole city of Seattle knows whom you were talking about."

"I doubt that. Only those who know us would understand. Here, won't you sit down?"

Pastor strode across the room and lowered his long frame onto the sofa while I sat on a chair opposite him.

"By the way, where's Agnes?" the pastor asked, his eyes narrowing.

"She went to a bridal shower tonight."

"I assume she did most of the writing. If she felt this way, why didn't you bring her in to see me so we could talk about it?"

I looked back at him and said, "I wouldn't do that to her. I've heard what happens when people question you, especially women. You intimidate them and send them out crying."

"Don't be ridiculous." He suddenly sat up and rested his

elbows on his neat, gray slacks. Punctuating his words with a waggling forefinger, he snapped, "I demand a retraction in the next issue of your paper. And if you don't—I'll bring out all the elders and *make* you do it."

With that, he jumped up and strode out the door.

I was too shaken to move. I stared at the closed door and listened to the powerful engine roaring up the street.

Just then, the long tablecloth wiggled, and Kenny crawled out of hiding. "Hey, Dad, you did a great job!" he yelled.

I blinked at our bright-eyed son. "What were you doing under there?"

"Listening. I wanted to hear what was going on. I was rootin' and praying for you."

"Great!" I grinned and hugged him. "I needed it."

"Wait'l Mom hears about this." Kenny laughed as he played with Blackie, our wiggly cock-a-poo. They hadn't had so much excitement for a long time.

About 9:30 that evening, Agnes drove up to our home nestled among birch and fir trees. Kenny ran to her in his blue football pajamas when she opened the door.

"Mom, guess what?"

"What?"

"Pastor was here."

"Oh, no. What did he want?"

"Something about that article you wrote. I hid under the table and heard it all. Pastor was real mad, but Dad was real cool. He answered him right back—nicely, though."

"Really? Let's tuck you in bed now. You've got school tomorrow, remember."

After praying with our son and kissing him good night, we returned to the living room.

I pulled Agnes down beside me on the sofa and gave her the details of the encounter. "I'm worried about Pastor bringing the elders out," I said with a frown.

"What can they do? They can't excommunicate us because we've already left the church. I think he's trying to intimidate us into publishing a retraction."

"I'm sure of that." I looked at her with concern. "Aren't you afraid?"

"Not really. Before we wrote that article, I felt the Lord ask, 'Are you willing to go to the cross for me? Will you suffer a little if you can help free my imprisoned sheep?'"

She told how she had gulped and finally said, "Yes, Lord. I'm willing. Just give me the words and the strength to bear whatever comes."

"You know," she continued. "I haven't been out of the house on a weeknight for months on end since we left the church. The hurt is still raw. But on this particular evening when I went to a family shower, Pastor came, so I didn't have to see him. The Lord is good, isn't he?"

"He sure is." I pulled her towards me for a hug.

When we finally went to bed, I dropped right off to sleep as usual. But Agnes lay awake thinking about our strange adventure with that aberrant Christian church.

About ten years later, because of numerous abuses, the elder board of that church told the senior pastor to refrain from the teaching and practices of shepherding. When he refused they asked him to resign. He left for a branch church, taking some three hundred members with him.

## Questions

1. Of what value can prayer be in making major decisions?
2. What is wrong with confrontation as practiced in the shepherding movement?
3. In an authoritarian structure, why is independence of thought and action decried?
4. Why is leaving a close, authoritarian group traumatic?
5. How can that trauma and depression be stopped?

# Chapter 3

# Going with the Flow

Consciousness of the past alone
can make us understand the present.
                        —Herbert Luethy

In the early 1970s, one hundred of "God's special people" sold their property, gave the money to their leader, and formed a 70-acre farm commune outside a small town in western Washington State. By 1979, authorities convicted the leader of rape, indecent liberties with minors, coercion, and assault. He spent six years in prison. The group disbanded— disillusioned, impoverished, and bitter.

In the 1980s, a three-thousand-member church in a Seattle, Washington, suburb began a "new move of God"—dancing with partners of the opposite sex (not their spouses) during worship services. These partners became "spiritual connections" to "show God's love" to one another. Result? Adultery, divorce, incest, child sexual abuse, suicide, murder.

Even worse, members of the Branch Davidian sect near Waco, Texas, claimed their polygamous leader, David Koresh, was Christ. On February 28, 1993, to "protect" their commune, they killed four federal agents and wounded sixteen others. On April 19, some apparently set the fires that turned into a blazing inferno, killing all who stayed inside.

In addition, critics charge some present-day televangelists with fraudulent actions—claiming erroneous needs, making false promises of healing and prosperity, using donated money lavishly on themselves rather than on claimed missionary ministries.

Christian cult-watchers claim these and other televangelists and preachers of the faith movement are teaching heresy—a deistic view of God, a demonic view of Christ, a gnostic view of revelation, a metaphysical view of salvation, and the deification of man.

In each case, these groups and leaders began in evangelical Christian traditions.

In the light of such aberrant teachings and practices, we may well ask, Is it possible for an evangelical Christian church to drift into deception and heresy? Can a strong spiritual leader go astray?

One look at church history will tell us it is not only possible, but it has happened time and again. In fact, many false cults have sprung from Christian roots.

Authors and researchers Flo Conway and Jim Siegelman agree. In a report of their extensive questionnaires sent to ex-cult members, they say, "Thirty of the forty-eight cults we surveyed emerged out of this traditional branch of Christianity."[1]

## What is an Aberrant Christian Group?

What do we mean by an *aberrant* Christian organization? How does it differ from a cult or from evangelical Christianity? From where does it come?

We may define an aberrant group as *one which emerged from orthodox, mainstream Christianity, but differs from it in belief and practice in one or more essential ways.* The word *aberrant* means "straying from the right or normal way; deviating from the usual or natural type."

An aberrant Christian group, then, is neither a cult nor an evangelical organization. Cult-watcher Robert M. Bowman, Jr., formerly of the Christian Research Institute, clarifies the difference between the three.

He says that a group is *heretical* "if it errs by denying one or more of the essentials" of orthodox Christian doctrine, such as the virgin birth or the deity of Christ. It is *aberrant* "if it compromises or confuses the essentials, without negating them," he says. It is *orthodox* [evangelical] "if it soundly affirms the essentials, whatever it may teach on nonessentials."[2]

## From Where Does an Aberrant Group Come?
In our definition, we said that an aberrant group emerges from orthodox, mainstream Christianity. Since history repeats itself, let us look at some leaders who began well, but led their followers first into aberration, then into outright heresy.

### Children of God
One example is the founder of the Children of God, David Brandt Berg. His father was a pastor for many years and later taught at Westmont College, a Christian school in Santa Barbara, California. His mother was a radio evangelist. Berg also became an evangelist in 1941,[3] then pastored an evangelical church in Valley Farms, Arizona, between 1948 and 1951. When he was asked to leave over doctrinal differences, he taught at several Christian schools and worked with evangelist Fred Jordan for thirteen years.

In 1967, Berg began an independent ministry called "Teens for Christ" among the "hippies" in Huntington Beach, California. At this time, he emphasized Bible study, Scripture memorization, and purity of life.[4]

The group has gradually evolved into a large, international organization. To maintain control, Berg calls himself "Moses" and uses dictatorial power to promote "liberty in Christ." This liberty expresses itself in heavy drinking and sexual perversions.[5]

Berg not only holds his own writings—"'Mo' Letters"— as above Scripture, but he rejects those parts of the Bible that contradict his teachings. He denies the biblical doctrines of God, Christ, and the Holy Spirit and even blasphemously imputes sexual perversions to them.[6]

### The Way International
A similar case in point is the late Victor Paul Wierwille, founder of The Way International. Raised in a Christian home, Wierwille graduated from Mission House College and Seminary at Plymouth, Wisconsin. He studied at the University of Chicago and received a master's degree in practical theology from Princeton Theological Seminary in New Jersey. In 1941, he was ordained a minister in the Evangelical and Reformed Church (now United Church of Christ) and pastored a church in Payne, Ohio, for a time.[7]

After he established The Way International, now with
some fifty thousand active members, he denied the biblical
doctrines of the Trinity, the nature of God, and the deity of
Christ and the Holy Spirit. He taught that salvation is
attained only through vocal confession of faith and speaking
in tongues.[8]

## The Branch Davidians

Sixteen federal agents wounded. Four others killed. Some
eighty-four members' lives lost when their commune went
up in billowing, black smoke and orange flames.

Oddly enough, this bizarre group sprang from what many
consider evangelical Christian roots. It began with an
emigrant from Bulgaria, Victor Houteff, a member of a Los
Angeles Seventh-Day Adventist Church. Hungering for
renewal, he developed "divergent views," then shared them
with other members. Church leaders disfellowshipped him
in 1929-30.

After self-publishing two books, *The Shepherd's Rod, Vol. 1*
and *Vol. 2,* Houteff led twelve followers to Mount Carmel,
Texas, in 1935. He proclaimed himself as "David" who would
establish his kingdom in Jerusalem with the 144,000 elect.
Houteff cut his ties with the mainstream church and formed
the Davidian Seventh-Day Adventist Association in 1942.
For the next twenty years, the group grew to ten thousand
members worldwide, with some 125 living at Mount Carmel.

Victor Houteff died in 1955, and his wife Florence took
over as leader. She proclaimed April 22, 1959, as the
beginning of end-time judgments, the removal of Jews and
Arabs from Palestine, the formation of the Davidic kingdom,
and the possible second coming of Christ.

One thousand followers sold their assets, gave the money
to the church, and gathered at Mount Carmel to await these
exciting events. When nothing happened, disillusioned
members left the Davidian movement or joined other
splinter factions. Houteff's group virtually ceased to exist
by the late 1960s.

The largest splinter group, the Branch Davidians, was led
by Benjamin Roden and stayed at Mount Carmel. When he
died in 1978, his wife Lois took charge, calling herself "the
incarnation of the Holy Spirit."

She died in 1986, and their son George became leader as

"the divinely appointed messenger of God." He later called himself "the messiah" and "the son of Christ."

Its recent leader, David Koresh (born Vernon Howell), attended a Tyler, Texas, Seventh-Day Adventist Church until he was disfellowshipped for getting the pastor's fifteen-year-old daughter pregnant. He drifted to the Branch Davidian compound in 1981.

Twenty-one-year-old Koresh ingratiated himself into leadership ranks by having a lengthy affair with Lois Roden, who was some forty years older. She allowed him to do some teaching of the group.

When Koresh claimed to be "inspired of God" in 1983, a rivalry began with Lois' son George. In 1985, Koresh moved to Palestine, Texas, where he was joined by several other members. They lived in plywood and cardboard shacks until the rivalry exploded into a gunfight in 1987, a year after Lois' death.

It ended with Roden spending six months in jail, leaving Koresh and his followers to take over the Branch Davidian compound.

Before long, Koresh claimed to be Jesus Christ reincarnated, the Lamb of Revelation, David, and King Cyrus (*Koresh* is the Hebrew for Cyrus). He taught that God is a foursome—Father, Mother (the Holy Spirit), Son, and Daughter (Holy Ghost). The Daughter will be Koresh's eternal mate when he is "glorified." Meantime, all females, single and married, in the compound were his "wives," some as young as ten years old.

Koresh subjected members to "beatings, sexual abuse, emotional trauma, mental torture, and spiritual ruin."[9]

These groups started out well with roots in traditional, evangelical Christianity. Yet along the way, the leaders drifted into aberrant, then heretical beliefs and practices, taking their followers with them.

The frightening question is, Could this happen to us and to our churches or groups?

## Watch Those Warning Signs!

Fog enfolded our car like a gray blanket as we slowly drove down a narrow, winding road. Out of the mist, an orange sign appeared, saying "MEN WORKING." As we crept along, we saw other signs—"LANE CLOSED" and "FLAGMAN AHEAD."

Then through dense fog, rotating lights blinked atop road equipment. An orange-vested flagman held up a stop sign and waved cars through from the opposite direction. We waited until he signaled us to move again.

We could have ignored the warning signs and barreled our way through, but such behavior could have resulted in an accident or loss of life.

Just as it pays to heed warning signs in our natural lives, it pays to watch for them in our spiritual lives as well. God warns us in both church history and Scripture regarding false teaching. We need to combine a study of the two to have these signs stand out for us in bold "technicolor."

How can an evangelical group drift into heresy? To answer, we'll look at both historical records and Scripture throughout the rest of the book.

But first we'll give you a brief summary of characteristics which aberrant leaders and organizations have in common.

## Common Characteristics of Aberrant Leaders and Groups

*Leadership*

1. *The leader has charisma and pride.* An aberrant leader uses his magnetic personality, his hypnotic eyes, and his powers of persuasion to attract and hold people to himself.

2. *The leader is angry with those who disagree.* Any follower who questions or disagrees with his teaching becomes the target of his anger and intimidation. The "rebel" must either repent and submit or else leave the group in disgrace.

3. *The leader is greedy and fraudulant.* The leader urges his people to give more and more to his group. In time, he may use fraud to extract vast amounts of money from unsuspecting victims.

A commune leader often insists that incoming members turn their assets into cash and give it to him. He lives on a higher—often luxurious—level than his people.

4. *The leader may become immoral.* An aberrant leader may teach that God has given him a "new revelation" regarding sexual relationships. He and they can show the "love of Christ" through immoral practices.

*Structure*

1. *An aberrant group has an enslaving authoritarian structure.*

With an organization shaped like a pyramid, the leader controls a network of assistants. Each assistant, in turn, exercises excessive control over the personal lives of his people.

*2. An aberrant group is exclusive.* It cuts itself off from those who disagree with its doctrinal stance. It has little or no fellowship with other churches in the evangelical community and may form a commune to isolate members from the outside world.

*3. An aberrant group demands loyalty and honor.* This may be in the form of "covenant commitments" made verbally or in writing, where members submit themselves to the leader. He uses various types of abuse to maintain loyalty and honor to him and to the group.

## Teaching

*1. An aberrant leader claims to have "new," extrabiblical revelation.* The leader feels God has revealed something special to him, something never before revealed to mankind, truths which supersede all previous teachings. Or he thinks he has the ability to reinterpret Scripture like no one else.

We will be discussing these eight warning signs in more detail in the remainder of the book.

Briefly, they are:

- Charisma and pride
- Anger and intimidation
- Greed and fraud
- Immorality
- Enslaving authoritarian structure
- Exclusivity
- Demands loyalty and honor
- "New" extrabiblical revelation

## Why Warn?

Cult-watchers Conway and Siegelman explain: "Cults in America are wreaking havoc on the minds and lives of millions . . . . But in the eloquent testimony of these hundreds of former cult members, . . . there is a plea for help that should not be ignored."[10]

After leaving our former church in 1979, we have encountered other victims who have come out of similar groups. They too are so traumatized that they take years to recover.

Many are unable to concentrate or make decisions for themselves. They are fearful of getting involved in other churches; some give up attending church at all. Most go through emotional upsets similar to the grief process following death or divorce. Some experience nervous breakdowns. A few even commit suicide or murder.

Because of this, we feel that Christians need the apostle Paul's warnings today more than ever. He grieved over error slipping into the early church. In his farewell to the Ephesian elders, he warned, "I know that after I leave, savage wolves will come in among you and will not spare the flock. Even from your own number men will arise and distort the truth in order to draw away disciples after them. So be on your guard! Remember that for three years I never stopped warning each of you night and day with tears" (Acts 20:29-31).

Paul also spent a good portion of his letters to Timothy warning against false doctrine. The apostle Peter, too, devoted most of his second letter cautioning believers about heresy creeping into the church. The apostle John did likewise in his epistles. Moreover, most of Jude's short epistle is a harsh warning.

Let's heed these warnings and guard ourselves and our groups from drifting into deception.

## Questions
1. Why is it important to study church history?
2. Explain the differences between these three: an orthodox group, an aberrant group, and a heretical group.
3. From where does an aberrant Christian group come?
4. Give some characteristics of an aberrant leader, an aberrant structure, and aberrant teaching.
5. What scriptural basis do we have for warning of aberration and heresy?

# Part II:
# Eight Warning Signs

# Chapter 4

# Charisma and Pride

Of all the causes which conspire to blind
Man's erring judgment, and misguide the mind,
What the weak head with strongest bias rules,
Is pride, the never-failing vice of fools.
—Alexander Pope

### Charisma

Adolf Hitler's charisma vaulted him into a place of power in Germany between the Great Wars. But in the spring of 1931, his "storm troopers" revolted against him.

He quickly deposed their leader, then ordered them all to appear in Berlin's Sportpalast for a roll call. In the silence of that vast arena, Hitler's heels clicked like castanets as he paced off columns of solemn, uniformed men.

Young Albert Speer, a member of an affiliate group, froze at attention in his squadron.

At last, Hitler came to his row. The fuehrer stared at each man in turn, willing a vow of loyalty.

Speer says, "When he came to me, I had the feeling that a pair of staring eyes had taken possession of me."[1]

This was Speer's first encounter with Hitler, but it was not his last. He went on to become the leader's personal architect, confidant, and protege. Hitler appointed him Reich minister for armaments and war production. By the end of World War II, he emerged as the second most powerful man in Nazi Germany.

What was so compelling about Hitler? Neither tall nor handsome, he was even a little knock-kneed. His face was coarse with a large nose and thick nostrils. Journalist and author William L. Shirer has an answer:

It was the eyes that dominated the otherwise common face. They were hypnotic. Piercing. Penetrating.

What hit you at once was their power. They stared at you. They stared through you. They seemed to immobilize the person on whom they were directed, frightening some and fascinating others, especially women, but dominating them in any case . . . . I would observe hardened old party leaders, who had spent years in the company of Hitler, freeze as he paused to talk to one or the other of them, hypnotized by his penetrating glare.[2]

Another characteristic that enhanced Hitler's charisma was his power of oratory. Shirer, who spent years as a correspondent in Berlin, heard most of his major speeches. He writes:

His oratory also was overwhelming, at least to Germans. It held them spellbound . . . . It was Hitler's eloquence, his astonishing ability to move a German audience by speech, that more than anything else had swept him from oblivion to power as dictator.[3]

When Hitler spoke, he "established a rapport almost immediately" with his audience. This intensified until he held people completely under his spell. He could make them believe anything, even what seemed to Shirer as "utter rubbish" and "brazen lies."[4]

Hitler's "personal magnetism," coupled with his hypnotic gaze and eloquence, held his followers "in his grip."[5] Together, they were the secret of his charisma.

Charisma in itself is not wrong, of course. Many people have used it for the glory of God. Pastor Peter Marshall, for instance, used his magnetic personality to glorify Christ. Emigrating from Scotland to America as a poor youth, he eventually became the eminent minister of New York Avenue Presbyterian Church in Washington, D. C. and chaplain for the United States Senate.

Tall and powerfully built, he preached with golden tongue and picturesque rhetoric that enthralled audiences. People lined up for hours on Sunday mornings to get seats for his services. Yet his wife, Catherine Marshall, felt he was one of the humblest men she knew.

Jesus certainly had charisma while on earth, but he did not use it for his own ends. His aim was to glorify his Father. After he fed the five thousand, the crowd wanted to make him king. But he quietly slipped away rather than accept earthly glory (see John 6:15).

In contrast, when a leader uses his penetrating eyes, his gifts of oratory, and his magnetic personality for his own ends, he becomes dangerous. Like a skilled violinist, he plays upon the emotions of his audience, swaying them with the melody of his words. His people hold him in awe and follow him blindly. To them, he is king.

Like Hitler, three characteristics compose the compelling charm of an aberrant leader—penetrating eyes, persuasive speech, and a dynamic personality. He attracts followers with his gift of oratory, his air of authority, and his idealistic goals.

One of today's prominent examples of charisma used the wrong way is the hero of the Unification Church, Korean-born Sun Myung Moon. Professor and author Ronald Enroth tells about a young girl who worked as housekeeper in one of the church's mansions. When Moon planned a visit, this girl worked nonstop for three months to prepare for his coming. So great was her love for him that she was beside herself for joy.

When Moon finally walked into the house, the young lady felt blown against the wall by his magnetic presence. He seemed surrounded by an awesome, invisible force that was overwhelming. After Moon left, all the things that he had touched or used were divided up among members like sacred artifacts.[6]

Another case in point is the leader of a commune in western Washington. After training at a Bible institute in New York State, he moved west and held Bible studies in Seattle and Bellevue, Washington.

"I've never heard such marvelous teaching," middle-aged Peggy told us. "The presence of the Lord was so real that we sat in silent awe after the meetings."

As his reputation increased, people jammed into homes to hear him teach. They were swayed by his oratory, hypnotized by his gaze, mesmerized by his personality.

Gradually, however, the leader used that force to exercise control over his followers. He urged them to sell their homes for a farm commune, and many did so. Even when he allegedly abused them by mishandling their money and leading them into sexual misconduct, they obeyed him unquestioningly as though he were God.

### Pride

The leader of an aberrant Christian group not only has charisma, but also arrogant pride.

Pride is the peril of the pinnacle position. It also is the mother of deception. It enticed Lucifer to stage a coup in heaven with his declaration, "I will make myself like the Most High" (Isa. 14:14). When Lucifer fell and became Satan, he dangled the promise of divinity like a glittering crystal in front of Eve. He enticed her to taste forbidden fruit with his promise, "You will be like God" (Gen. 3:5).

A leader may begin his ministry with a heart for the Lord and a desire to serve him. In true humility, he teaches what he receives from God's Word, and his people are blessed.

As his group grows and gives him praise, however, pride often creeps in. Because of the demands of his growing ministry and an increasing self-confidence, he spends less time with the Lord and his Word. He no longer gives God all the glory. He fails to confess pride as sin; he fails to ask for humility. Instead, he takes to himself adulation meant only for the Almighty.

As the poet S. T. Coleridge aptly wrote:

> And the Devil did grin,
> For his darling sin
> Is pride that apes humility.[7]

Critics see the same pride developing in evangelical "superstars" today. One televangelist recently said, "Those that mess with me, they're messing with the apple of God's eye!"[8]

The leader of the commune referred to earlier called himself "Michael" the archangel so often that his people believed he was the angel incarnated. He even implied that he was God himself when he read Scripture verses such as John 14:9, "Don't you know me . . . even after I have been among you such a long time?" He then closed the Bible and stood quietly in the reverent gazes of his people.

The founder and pastor of a church and Bible school in Burien, Washington, claims he had a visionary experience in the "throne room" of heaven where he was "connected" with God and became "one essence" with Jesus.

David Koresh of the Branch Davidians claimed he was not only the biblical David and King Cyrus, but also he was the Lamb of Revelation and Jesus Christ reincarnated. As such, he was the only one who could interpret Scripture.[9]

## What God Says About Pride
*1. God tells us not to idolize people.* He says, "Worship the Lord your God, and serve him only" (Matt. 4:10). "I am the Lord; that is my name! I will not give my glory to another" (Isa. 42:8).

A graphic illustration of one who took God's glory to himself is in Acts chapter twelve. When King Herod spoke before a large audience with great eloquence, his listeners cried, "This the voice of a god, not of a man!" (v. 22).

As Herod basked in their praise, the angel of the Lord struck him with a loathsome disease. He died because he took the glory to himself instead of giving it to God (Acts 12:21–24).

*2. God hates pride.* The Lord says, "Whoever has haughty eyes and a proud heart, him will I not endure" (Ps. 101:5). "God opposes the proud but gives grace to the humble" (1 Pet. 5:5).

One of the most colorful examples of pride in the Bible is the story of Haman, prime minister of the vast Medo-Persian empire. When King Xerxes gave him this position, he commanded all royal officials to kneel before Haman every time he passed by. They complied—all except Mordecai the Jew. This made Haman furious. Mordecai made him "lose face," an unthinkable affront to the Oriental mind.

Therefore, Haman sought revenge not just on Mordecai alone, but on all his people throughout the empire. The proud, crafty prime minister flattered the king and promised 375 tons of silver for the royal treasury for the privilege of destroying these "different" people. So the edict went forth, and the judgment day was set.

When Queen Esther invited only the king and Haman to a banquet, the prime minister's pride was further inflated. He held a "brag party" that evening for his friends and family. He boasted of his vast wealth. His numerous sons. His promotion above all other officials. His invitation to the queen's private party. His entry into the inner circle of royalty.

But Haman was not satisfied with his position of glory as long as one man refused to bow to him. At the suggestion of his wife and friends, he built a gallows seventy-five feet high on which to hang Mordecai the next day.

God, however, opposed this proud leader. That night the Lord arranged to have record books read to the king and a good deed of Mordecai brought to light. In the morning, the king ordered Haman to clothe the Jew in royal robes and lead him through the city streets on a royal horse. Worse yet, he had to proclaim, "This is what is done for the man the king delights to honor!"

When the truth of Haman's treachery came out at Queen Esther's second banquet, Haman toppled from his pinnacle of power. She pointed him out as the instigator of the plot to kill her and her people.

Furious, King Xerxes condemned Haman to hang on the gallows prepared for Mordecai. And he gave Mordecai Haman's position.

Haman's enormous vice of pride showed him for what he was—a fool.

3. *God will punish the proud.* The Bible says, "Pride goes before destruction, a haughty spirit before a fall" (Prov. 16:18).

Scripture gives examples of godly people who started out on track, but became filled with pride. It led to their deception and downfall every time.

One such example was a good king of Judah, Uzziah, (see 2 Chron. 26:1–23). As a young man, he obeyed Zechariah, the godly high priest "who instructed him in the fear of God." Result? "As long as he sought the Lord, God gave him success" (v. 5). In time, his military might increased and his fame spread. Everything he did was first-class.

Gradually, pride crept into his heart. "After Uzziah became powerful, his pride led to his downfall" (v. 16).

One day he went into the temple to burn incense on the altar. Azariah, now high priest, with eighty other courageous priests, confronted him. "It is not right for you," Azariah said, "to burn incense to the Lord. That is for the priests, the descendants of Aaron, who have been consecrated."

Censer in hand, Uzziah glowered at them.

"Leave the sanctuary," they urged, "for you have been unfaithful; and you will not be honored by the LORD God."

Uzziah refused. As he raged at the priests in a burst of anger, leprosy broke out on his forehead. The horrified priests hustled him out of the sanctuary. This time he cooperated because he realized the Lord had punished him. Until the day of his death, Uzziah lived in isolation, relieved of his kingly responsibilities.

In contrast, leaders whom God has greatly used have humbled themselves and given him all the glory. Evangelist Dwight L. Moody was such a man. After preaching one evening during a citywide campaign, he learned that a group of influential people wished to meet him. Moody didn't hurry to greet them, but slipped quietly out the backdoor and to his room. Later, he explained why: "I feared to tarry for the words of adulation and flattery. I had to report first to my Lord who sent me forth."[10]

Consider these questions:

1. Does your church or group focus on your leader rather than Christ? Have you put him on a pedestal and indulged in hero worship? Are you swayed by his oratory, hypnotized by his gaze, mesmerized by his personality?

2. Is there evidence that your leader is proud and arrogant? Does he humbly confess his sins and inadequacies to the group?

3. Does your leader glorify God or himself when success comes? Does he place himself between his congregation and Christ?

Yes, we may want a hero, but let's make sure that hero is Jesus Christ.

## Questions

1. What personal characteristics propelled Hitler to power?
2. What three aspects of charisma can be dangerous?
3. What three things does God say about pride?
4. Describe Haman's pride. How did God bring him down from his lofty perch?
5. Why did good King Uzziah deserve punishment?

# Chapter 5

# Anger and Intimidation

A man's venom poisons himself
More than his victim.
—Charles Buxton

During World War II as news from the German fronts grew worse, Adolf Hitler was convinced that his orders were being disobeyed. He confronted his chief of staff General Heinz Guderian on February 13, 1945. Hitler stood with "his fists raised, his cheeks flushed with rage, his whole body trembling." With each outburst, the general said his leader "was almost screaming, his eyes seemed to pop out of his face, and the veins stood out in his temples."[1]

Hitler, of course, is not the only leader who vented his wrath when crossed or disobeyed. We see it today in aberrant Christian groups.

A recent example is the infamous David Koresh of the Branch Davidians. Koresh hadn't been at their commune long before sparks flew between him and leader George Roden, who claimed to be a "divinely appointed messenger of God"—in fact, the "messiah" and the "son of Christ."

Koresh also claimed to be "inspired of God." But he had a volatile temper. Like a lighted match to a barrel of gasoline, the rivalry soon erupted into conflict. He left for two years, taking some members with him.

The showdown came in 1987. Roden exhumed a body,

then challenged Koresh to resurrect it. Whoever could do so would be the acknowledged leader of the group.

Koresh and several armed followers made a night raid on the Branch Davidian compound, supposedly to take photos of the body.

Roden felt they were out to kill him. The conflict escalated into a shootout. Authorities arrested Koresh and seven of his men. The bizarre trial which followed resulted in Koresh and his followers being set free, while Roden was given a six-month jail sentence for threatening the justices of the Texas State Supreme Court.

When Roden was jailed in January 1988, Koresh and his followers took over the Branch Davidian compound. Former members report that the new leader often displayed his fiery temper. If children cried, he beat them until they were bruised and bleeding. If adult members "disobeyed" or questioned him, he beat them or deprived them of food and sleep. Koresh ruled the compound through fear and intimidation.[2]

Not all abuse in aberrant Christian groups is so dramatic. For instance, Ron was a respected elder in a shepherding church. After the pastor put himself under the headship of a famous Bible teacher, Ron was concerned.

He went to his pastor and said, "I feel uneasy about the shepherding teaching. Some of it seems questionable." He spoke quietly and lovingly.

The pastor, however, reacted with anger. "If you don't like the way things are going, you can leave!"

And Ron and his family left the church sorrowing.

A second warning sign of an aberrant leader is his anger when others disagree with him or question him. To intimidate his followers into obedience, he uses the weapons of verbal and physical abuse and threats of excommunication and eternal judgment.

## Weapons of Anger
*The Weapon of Verbal Abuse*

James, a middle-aged man in a shepherding church, went to his pastor with questions about his teaching and practices.

Result? The minister publicly condemned him in a Sunday morning service and removed him from all leadership positions. When James later tried to defend himself in a board meeting, the pastor shouted, "Sit down and be quiet!"

## The Weapon of Physical Abuse

The leader of a commune in western Washington had a prize disciple named Brenda. She joined the group as a teenager with an illegitimate baby named Jeremiah. Brenda had trouble making the boy mind, so the leader decided to teach the toddler how to obey.

One day the leader became angry when Jeremiah disobeyed. He forced the child to run around a table, around a chair, into the kitchen, into a closet, then crawl through the rungs of a small chair. The angry leader made him repeat this over and over.

When the women in the group gathered for a meeting on another occasion, the leader put Jeremiah through his paces to demonstrate his obedience, how he had "taken him over." The leader forced the boy to go through his routine so many times that the ladies grew tired of watching.

Every time little Jeremiah wet his bed or did something wrong, the leader made him go through this routine until he fell in exhaustion. Then he said, "Come over now and give me a kiss."

The toddler whimpered and cried like an animal, but he still had to comply.

To further punish Jeremiah, the leader put him in a closet for hours at a time. He once beat him so hard in a fit of anger that the child went unconscious. The leader and Brenda took him to a hospital and claimed he had fallen downstairs.

When Jeremiah came out of his coma three days later, one of his eyes went to the right and the other to the left. The doctors felt he had suffered brain damage.

## The Fear of Excommunication

Tim and Judy's lives centered on their community church in Burien, a suburb south of Seattle, Washington. After ten loyal years, they left over ethical questions and were "disfellowshipped." Relatives in the church refused to speak to them; once-close friends ignored them. They felt as if they had gone through the trauma of a divorce. Although disfellowshipping required relatives to relinquish only spiritual fellowship, it resulted, however, in completely broken ties with all Tim and Judy's family and friends still in the church.

Both excommunication and defection are painful

experiences. As we discovered, people who leave these groups are cut off with little or no further contact. Members are ordered to have nothing to do with defectors, even members of their own families. If their whole social and spiritual lives have been tied up with the church and if their friends and family are still there, they find it particularly difficult.

### *The Fear of Eternal Judgment*

Leader Frank Sandford of a turn-of-the-century commune in Maine called Shiloh, for instance, publicly disciplined one of his "ministers." A young woman defended the latter. Almost beside himself with rage, Sandford shouted at her, saying that her sin was too great for forgiveness and that she was doomed to hell.

The young lady was so terrified that she became physically and emotionally ill and died two years later.[3]

## Rationale for Anger

An aberrant leader feels he as God's spokesman has a perfect right to get angry at his people.

For instance, Frank Sandford claimed this showed he was "one with God." In 1899 while preaching from Exodus 32, he said: "Do you suppose Moses was excusable for being angry? . . . When one with God, we feel as God feels; and when he is angry, we shall be angry. This little silly idea that if you have God in you, you will never be angry must go."

After speaking of the Levites taking up the sword against idol worshipers, Sandford said, "That is the spirit God wants in this Bible school. He wants you so true to God that there will not be the slightest pity or mercy shown to the man, woman, or child in this place that is not absolutely true to God."[4]

## What God Says About Anger

*1. God says not to sin when angry.* He states, "'In your anger do not sin': Do not let the sun go down while you are still angry" (Eph. 4:26).

God further says that a leader especially should not give way to anger: "Since an overseer is entrusted with God's work, he must be blameless—not overbearing, not quick-tempered, . . . not violent" (Titus 1:7).

Is there a place for "righteous indignation?" Of course. In the Bible, we see that God gets angry with sin. Christ became righteously angry when he saw money changers getting rich off their temple traffic and wealthy Pharisees defrauding poor widows and orphans. Yet in his anger, Jesus did not sin.

On the other hand, most of us have failed in this area. "The word of anger and hastiness of passion and temper," says evangelist and author Herbert Lockyer, "dog the footsteps of the best saints, giving them sorrow of heart and destroying their influence over others."[5]

Moses, Israel's leader out of Egypt and through the wilderness, was such a close friend that God spoke to him face to face. Yet almost at the end of his people's wanderings, Moses sinned by getting angry at them. They had arrived at the Desert of Zin—hot, tired, and thirsty. But no water was available for them or their livestock.

Forgetting how God had provided for them in the past, angry leaders confronted Moses. "If only we had died when our brothers fell dead before the Lord! . . . Why did you bring us up out of Egypt to this terrible place? It has no grain, no figs, no grapevines, no pomegranates. And there is no water!"

Moses and Aaron turned away without a word. They went into the Tent of Meeting and fell on their faces before God.

"Take the staff, and . . . gather the assembly together," the Lord said. "Speak to that rock before their eyes and it will pour out its water. You will bring water out of the rock for the community so they and their livestock can drink."

So Moses and Aaron gathered all the people together in front of the rock. But the two leaders were disgusted with the constant grumbling of the Israelites. "Listen, you rebels," Moses yelled in the heat of anger, "must we bring you water out of this rock?" He raised his staff high and struck the rock with two resounding blows. Water gushed out, enough for all the people and their livestock.

But God was grieved with his servant. Moses had sinned by losing his temper. Because he struck the rock instead of speaking to it, he had dishonored the Lord before the people. Therefore God said, "You will not bring this community into the land I give them." What a disappointment after forty hot, tiring years in the desert! God forgave, but he still punished (Num. 20:1–13).

2. *God says to get rid of anger.* He tells us, "Get rid of all

bitterness, rage and anger, brawling and slander, along with every form of malice" (Eph. 4:31).

Although we may call our anger "righteous indignation," God warns us not to indulge in it: "Everyone should be quick to listen, slow to speak and slow to become angry" (James 1:19–20).

In one of Jesus' parables, we have a graphic illustration of a man who nursed his anger instead of getting rid of it. The prodigal son returned home in tears of repentance. His delighted father dressed him in an elegant robe, put a ring on his finger, and slipped sandals on his feet. He ordered a feast prepared to celebrate the homecoming.

Meanwhile, the elder brother walked toward home after working all day in the fields. As he drew near, he heard music, laughter, and dancing. "What's going on?" he asked a servant.

"Your brother has come, and your father has killed the fatted calf because he has him back safe and sound."

"Of all the nerve!" we can imagine the older son saying. "Well, you won't catch me going in to welcome him—after what he's done." He turned away, muttering to himself and burning with anger.

Even when his father came out and pleaded with him to come to the party, he refused. "Look!" He spat the words. "All these years I've been slaving for you and never disobeyed your orders. Yet you never gave me even a young goat so I could celebrate with my friends. But when this son of yours who has squandered your property with prostitutes comes home, you kill the fattened calf."

"My son," the father said gently, tears pooling in his eyes, "you are always with me, and everything I have is yours. But we had to celebrate and be glad, because this brother of yours was dead and is alive again; he was lost and is found" (Luke 15:21–31).

The older son had probably banked coals of anger in the furnace of his heart for a long time. Was the joyful reception of his younger brother the bellows that fanned the coals into red-hot flames?

The parable does not tell us what happened to this brother. We can only hope that he joined his family in celebration and was able to forgive.

3. *God says anger produces trouble and strife.* Anger is

detrimental to our spiritual lives, "for man's anger does not bring about the righteous life that God desires" (James 1:20). Family counselor Craig Massey says, "How well he controls this powerful force [anger] is a good measure of a man's spiritual maturity."[6]

In fact, anger produces nothing but trouble. The Lord states, "A hot-tempered man stirs up dissension" (Prov. 15:18). Again, he says, "For as churning the milk produces butter, and as twisting the nose produces blood, so stirring up anger produces strife" (Prov. 30:33).

Anger also gives "the devil a foothold" in our lives (Eph. 4:27). Former missionary and author John A. MacMillan feels that anger indulged in over a period of time can make room for demonic spirits to influence a person. He says, "There is an intimate connection between sinful anger and the prince of evil, and sustained wrath will surely open the door to his entrance."[7]

When we see that evidenced, we can take authority over excessive anger that is demonically inspired. One evening, MacMillan and his wife heard another couple quarreling heatedly. Alarmed, they quietly "took authority over the spirits of evil who were behind the ostensible cause, and commanded their withdrawal. Almost immediately, the quarreling stopped."

MacMillan gives the secret of this authority: "A firm and positive refusal that the enemy shall have any right to work in the life, or the body, or the circumstances, will bring the foe to a standstill. And, as this attitude is maintained in quiet faith, a change will come, and the attacks will lose their force."[8]

*4. God says he will judge anger:* "Anyone who is angry with his brother will be subject to judgment . . . . Anyone who says, 'You fool!' will be in danger of the fire of hell" (Matt. 5:22).

Saul, the first king of Israel, is a vivid example of one whose all-consuming anger resulted in judgment. Because of Saul's continual disobedience, God sent an evil spirit to torment him (1 Sam. 16:14). The Holy Spirit departed from him and anointed David instead.

As a result, Saul became insanely jealous of David and indulged in angry outbursts. More than once he threw his lance at the younger man in an attempt to pin him to the wall.

Saul's anger even flared up at his son Jonathan. "You son

of a perverse and rebellious woman!" he shouted. "Don't I know that you have sided with the son of Jesse to your own shame? . . . As long as the son of Jesse lives on this earth, neither you nor your kingdom will be established. Now send and bring him to me, for he must die!"

"Why should he be put to death?" Jonathan asked. "What has he done?"

In answer, Saul hurled his spear at Jonathan, intending to kill him (1 Sam. 20:30–33). From then on, Saul's burning anger drove him to chase David through the wilderness and mountains of Israel.

Later, Philistine forces again invaded the land. When God refused to answer his prayers for direction, Saul felt he had no other recourse than to turn to satanic powers through the witch of Endor. Pressed by enemy forces, he fell on his own sword and committed suicide. The Philistines cut off his head, hung his armor in the temple of their gods, and fastened his body to a wall (1 Sam. 31:1–10).

One sad aspect of this story is that Jonathan, his two brothers, and Saul's valiant men died along with him. That's why the Lord warns us not to be under an angry leader: "Do not make friends with a hot-tempered man, do not associate with one easily angered, or you may learn his ways and get yourself ensnared" (Prov. 22:24–25).

If a leader persists in the sins of anger and intimidation, we should leave his group—lest we be caught in the judgment that is sure to come.

## Questions

1. What four weapons of anger can an aberrant leader use?
2. What rationale does he use for his anger?
3. Is there a place for "righteous indignation?" Explain.
4. What four things does God say about anger?
5. Why was Moses not allowed to enter the promised land?
6. What should we do when confronted with diabolically inspired anger?
7. Why should we leave a leader who indulges in anger?

# Chapter 6

# Greed and Fraud

There is within the human heart
a tough fibrous root of fallen life
whose nature is to possess, always to possess.
It covets "things" with a deep
and fierce passion.

—A. W. Tozer

Fourteen fur coats. An air-conditioned dog house. Six luxurious homes. Gold-plated bathroom fixtures. Fifty-foot walk-in closets. Yearly salaries of $1.9 million. Millions more for luxury autos, clothes, bodyguards, and private secretaries.

The leader and his wife resigned from their large television ministry in North Carolina, and the news hit the headlines in early 1987. The unprecedented scandal riveted the attention of the nation and rocked the Christian world.

Investigative reporters pulled aside the curtain of secrecy surrounding their operations. They revealed that these leaders had siphoned off millions of dollars to support their lavish living.

The wife explained part of the reason—her love of shopping. "It's kind of a hobby to help my nerves," she said in a television interview.[1]

After a sensational six-week trial, the husband was convicted on October 5, 1989, on twenty-four fraud, felony, and conspiracy charges. Of particular note was his "overselling subscriptions for a time-share scheme" at the huge theme park. "In return for $1,000, purchasers were entitled to three nights of lodging annually for the rest of their lives at a park hotel."[2]

A minister from Beavertown, Pennsylvania, testified that he paid for such a room and was unable to obtain a refund of the $1,000 fee. "I have a hard time dealing with the misuse of money," he said.[3]

On October 24, 1989, the leader was sentenced to forty-five years in federal prison and fined $500,000.[4]

Two years later, a US district judge ruled that the prison sentence be reduced to eighteen years.[5] The leader left a Georgia prison on July 1, 1994, after serving four-and-a-half years and moved to a Salvation Army halfway house in Asheville, North Carolina. Although he was released on December 1, 1994, he will remain under federal supervision through April 1997. While he was in prison, his wife divorced him and married another man.[6] He lives alone on a rented farm outside Hendersonville, North Carolina, where he is writing two books. On February 12, 1995, Jim Bakker came out of seclusion to preach at the funeral of a friend. The congregation of two thousand gave him two standing ovations.[7]

The third warning sign of an aberrant leader is greed and fraud. Not only is he proud and angry toward those who disagree, but he also loves money and what it can buy. This desire often results in fraudulent practices.

## Greed

Most pastors encourage their people to give tithes and offerings to support them and their churches, and this is scriptural.

An aberrant leader, however, goes a step further by controlling his people's giving. He makes sure that all tithes and offerings come his way. He checks on the giving records of his members and confronts them if he feels they are not giving enough. He discourages their supporting missions and other organizations outside his oversight. In a word, he is covetous.

The aberrant leader lives lavishly without the slightest bit of shame. After all, he's the "King's kid." Late author and pastor Jamie Buckingham asked a televangelist, "Why do you drive a $100,000 car?"

"A man in my kind of ministry needs good, solid transportation," the evangelist replied.[8]

He's not alone with this kind of thinking. In the late 1970s, a church in central Washington, was booming. It had a congregation of one thousand members, a choir of 150, a fifty-piece orchestra, and a ballet troupe. The church owned an FM radio station, East-West Films, and a video ministry making television specials. Its school system had over three hundred students. The church published a national magazine and established five branch churches in Washington State. Moreover, the church owned two large buses and a Cessna airplane to provide transportation around the country for its music ministries.[9]

The pastor's vision included acquiring a television station, a gymnasium, a performing-arts center, and a computer-marketing business. Apparently, he dreamed of even buying up the business section of the town.[10]

However, in March 1980, the whole operation was embroiled in a legal battle over money mismanagement. The business manager was charged with check fraud and stealing $350,000 from the church. He in turn "blamed the desires of the church's minister for his unorthodox money handling." According to the *Seattle Times*, the business manager claimed the pastor's "visions were so immense and the expenses so large . . . that finding the money to pay for them was often difficult."[11]

The business manager testified at the two-week trial that he often gave elaborate gifts to the pastor and his wife—a vacation cruise on the "Love Boat," expensive clothes, a new car for the pastor's mother, and a diamond ring for the pastor. An elder described him as "a cuff-link, patent-leather-shoe person." To do all this, however, the business manager admitted that he had obtained a $40,000 loan from a nightclub figure and racketeer.[12]

To account for his own actions, the business manager described his relationship with his pastor: "He told me we had a spiritual marriage, that I was Nehemiah and he was Moses . . . . I would have died for him. If he would have told me to jump off this building, I would have done it . . . . I submitted totally to the headship . . . . Anything he told me to go for, I took as his command, and I went for them."[13]

At the end of the trial, the former business manager was

acquitted by the jury on twelve counts of theft. Seattle First National Bank "began legal proceedings . . . to collect a $432,000 loan, plus interest, owed by [the church]." The church had to liquidate its gas station, bookstore, and radio station. It also closed its college, sold its buildings, and laid off most of its staff.[14]

Today this lifestyle is common among some other leaders. ABC's Diane Sawyer on "PrimeTime Live," (November 21, 1992) brought three examples of greed in Christian ministry to the public's attention.

Sawyer pointed out that a televangelist with a large church in Dallas, Texas, pled for money via his television program and direct mail. He claimed he only received a salary set by an "independent firm and one perk—a parsonage."

But he had three "parsonages," Sawyer revealed. One is a $4.5 million lakeside home in California "with pool, jacuzzis, thousands of dollars in furnishings, and a four-car garage for [his] Mercedes." He paid for the house in cash.

He also had a waterfront "parsonage" in Fort Lauderdale, Florida, where he docked a new $132,000 yacht. A third home was under construction in Texas, while he and his family rented a fourth house for $6,000 a month.

With himself as sole proprietor of his organization and only his wife and his secretary joining him on the board, the evangelist had direct access to $60 to $100 million in assets.[15]

Sawyer focused on a second televangelist who specializes in faith healing. At that time, he took in roughly "six million dollars" a year, according to an insider. While he "deposited some of the money in ministry bank accounts, he took out a portion for himself."

Astounded, Sawyer said to the worker, "I want to understand this correctly. Over the years, he has taken out, as his personal spending money, hundreds and hundreds of thousands of dollars?"

"Yes."

"What does he do with this money? Is he a big spender?"

"It would be nothing for him to spend $1,500 for a suit. He bought a Mercedes . . . for $32,000."

The cameras then zoomed in on a "million-dollar mansion" where he and his family live, just one of several properties that his ministry owns.[16]

The third televangelist included in "PrimeTime's" exposé had a 11,000-member church and lived on a palatial 5.1-acre estate outside Dallas. He had another beautiful home in Tulsa, Oklahoma—paid for in cash. We'll hear more of him in the next section.

## Fraud

An aberrant leader not only loves money and what it can buy, but he uses fraud to fund his visions and lifestyle.

For those who give, the leader makes false promises of spiritual and material rewards, answered prayers, and opportunities to help the poor. To make sure his followers give, he uses such things as free gifts, pressure, deceit, and threats.

All this has been done before. Perhaps the most flagrant example of greed and fraud in recent history was leader Jim Jones of the infamous People's Temple. He conned his followers into giving him millions of dollars.

How did Jones get the money? He told them to empty their savings accounts, to donate their jewelry and antiques, to sign over property deeds and insurance policies. He enforced tithing, demanding 25 percent of their incomes.[17]

## False Promises
### *Promises of Spiritual, Material, and Physical Rewards*

As a Marxist, Jim Jones preached to his followers that America was becoming a fascist country and would kill all African Americans or put them in concentration camps. It was only reasonable to give their all to the People's Temple so it could establish a utopia elsewhere before the fascists took it.

To assure them of his right to receive their assets as their "divine" leader, Jones supposedly displayed supernatural powers. He called individuals out of the congregation and told them personal things about themselves—where they came from, where they worked, who their parents were, and what medications they took. But insiders had previously sneaked into their homes, reading mail, noting prescription labels, and checking garbage.

Then Jones often took an offering lasting over an hour. He asked for large amounts first—five hundred dollars, then four hundred dollars and on down. People raised their hands

and deposited money or checks in baskets as ushers moved
up and down the aisles. One evening he made everyone write
checks for one hundred dollars before they could leave.[18]

The same tactics are used today. In a recent form letter, a
televangelist asked his followers to check off which "earthly
blessings" they wished to receive:

- Business breakthroughs
- Cars
- Clothes
- Favor with people
- Financial miracles
- Jobs
- Loans
- Tax problems solved
- Vacations

On another sheet, followers were to check off the
"heavenly blessings" they desired:

- Angelic protection
- Baptism of the Holy Spirit
- Divine direction
- Gift of faith
- Healing
- Hearing God's voice
- Prayer language released
- Spiritual growth
- Word of knowledge

The second step the televangelist asked the recipient to
take was "supernatural":

This is where faith is released, trust in God is expressed,
and seed is planted for the miracles of Heaven or earth that
you need. *This is it*: Sow a *supernatural* financial seed of faith
in this miracle soil of God. A supernatural seed is a financial
gift to God's work that is beyond what you would normally,
naturally give. *It is a gift that requires faith on your part to give.*
It requires you to trust God more than your
circumstances . . . more than your bank account
. . . more than what is comfortable. . . . It is something

supernatural! . . . *When you put anything into God's hands, you are opening yourself up for blessings that only he can give to you!*[19]

He then gave several testimonies of people who had experienced such rewards—doubled income, new houses, new jobs, physical healings.

One such false promise was made to a thirty-eight-year-old oil field truck driver in Tulsa, Oklahoma, who was incapacitated by diabetes. In a computerized letter, the televangelist wrote, "God spoke to me this morning specifically about you, Tom, and He's going to heal you." For a price, of course.

The truck driver made two contributions totaling seventy-five dollars to this ministry after watching the show. His income at that time was $435 a month in Social Security disability payments. He was convinced that God was going to heal him.

But he died of kidney failure on September 30, 1991.

His widow notified the televangelist's organization of the death.

Five months later, the faith healer was still sending letters addressed to the deceased, asserting that God had said he would heal him if he would send more money.

In February 1992, the widow sued the televangelist for forty million dollars in damages, saying that the letters caused her "anguish, shock, nervousness, and anxiety."[20] Another Oklahoma widow did the same.

Prompted by ABC's "PrimeTime Live" program, the Internal Revenue Service, the Federal Bureau of Investigation, the US postal inspector, and the Texas attorney general have been investigating this televangelist's operations.

Apparently he and his attorney of Tulsa, Oklahoma, shrug off the lawsuits, investigations, and media criticism as Satan's harrassments.[21]

## Promises of Prayers
The second trick Jones used was the promise of his prayers on behalf of contributors. He included a prayer cloth in each appeal letter with instructions to pin the cloth on one's clothing, to wear it for two days and nights, then to return it with a contribution and prayer requests.

Manipulations of this kind aren't the exception. Another evangelist, with the fastest-growing ministry on the air, had a "state-of-the-art 'factory' for donations," according to Diane Sawyer.

In a recent form letter, he wrote his followers: "I will literally take your *blessing desires* from *heaven* and anoint my hands with miracle anointing oil. I will then touch your requests and release my faith for your needs . . . and, just like Jesus did, I will touch them with a *second touch* while believing for your *double* portion of heavenly blessings."

He promised then to take the pages of "earthly blessing desires" people had sent in and lay his coat "(like a prophet's mantle)" upon them. He wrote, "I will pray that the anointing that flows from the prophetic ministry (that God has given me) will (by proxy) be placed upon you and your earthly desires."[22]

Included in this same mailing was a poster with a large picture of himself praying and holding the palm of his hand towards the camera. Underneath his photo is this note: "Touch my hands every day for 7 days . . . and cover your miracle needs with your prayers, and I will touch your prayer requests and release my faith again and again." (Here are two pictures of him on his knees with his suit jacket on top of papers, with the note: "Again and again.") "God told me," he continues, "to release my faith for your double blessing and second touch miracle."[23]

ABC investigators and the Trinity Foundation, a nonprofit watchdog group in Dallas, sifted through dumpsters at the televangelist's bank from August through October 1991. They found that "the majority of the prayer requests that [the leader] promises followers he'll personally and individually touch and pray over are routed first to a bank, then to a mail-processing facility, and finally to a recycling center—without the evangelist ever seeing them—*to be turned into toilet paper*" [original emphasis].[24]

## Promises to Help the Needy
Jones loved to take politicians, dignitaries, and other visitors on a tour of the temple's convalescent homes for elderly blacks and whites, a ranch for retarded children, and subsidized dormitories for poor college students in nearby Santa Rosa.[25]

At the time of ABC's expose, another televangelist raised thousands of dollars supposedly to support "3,500 children in sixty-four orphanages" in Haiti.

"For decades," Sawyer said, "he has touched hearts with televised appeals for food and clothes for orphans in Haiti."

In one clip, the televangelist showed two photographs to his televised audience. "This is an actual child in our Royal Palms Orphanage in Port-au-Prince, Haiti," he said. "Isn't this a beautiful child? Do you know that just four months before this picture was taken, she looked like this [shows picture of emaciated child]?"

But the second picture actually was of a different child in another country.

In his services, his associate pastor told the tear-jerking story of a "saintly woman" who ran one of the ministry's orphanages—a woman called "Mommy." But PrimeTime investigators found that "Mommy" had been dead for five years.

While in Haiti on the investigative mission, Sawyer met an American missionary who supposedly oversaw the "sixty-four orphanages."

This missionary said he was in charge of only one, with seventeen children. He claimed that the televangelist sent "a couple of thousand dollars a month."

But this televangelist was just one of those claiming this orphanage as their own. Apparently each one puts his own sign in front and has his picture taken with a couple of orphans.

Another service the missionary provided was "heart-tugging photos" of children for evangelists to use for fund-raising.[26]

A third televangelist featured in ABC's expose raised a large amount of money to build a church in Poland near a former Nazi concentration camp. The announcer on his television program said, "With the aid of a courageous local pastor, [the evangelist] is building the first Spirit-filled church in Auschwitz since the end of World War II."

"For six weeks," Sawyer said, "[his] phone lines lit up, taking donations for the cause."

*PrimeTime Live* investigators followed him undercover when he went to Poland. The church treasurer there told them that the building then standing "was started two years ago by the Polish Pentecostal community with money raised entirely on their own."

Before leaving Poland, the televangelist did give the church a one-time donation of thirty thousand dollars. "But," Sawyer added, "compared to the millions the . . . ministry takes in every year, a $30,000 gift is small change." She had obtained some of his bank records which showed that his ministry took in "more than a million dollars in one month."[27]

Another example of false promises to help the needy happened a few years ago in a small town in western Washington. The pastor of a growing church also headed a mission. He solicited money to support "needy orphans and native evangelists in Indonesia and other countries." In 1981, he was "indicted on 26 counts of defrauding the donors by diverting mission money to himself and his church."[28]

At the trial, several donors testified that they thought 100 percent of their donations went to support needy orphans and evangelists. The pastor had told them that "the mission paid no salaries and that overhead expenses were paid through separate offerings."[29]

Attorneys told the jury, however, that the pastor had purchased three cars, real estate, and personal items for himself. He also bought a carillon and electronic equipment for his church using mission checks—a total of $514,000 of the mission's money.[30]

## Means Used to Raise Money
*Free Gifts with Supernatural Powers*

Another trick Jim Jones played was the offer of "anointed" gifts with supernatural powers in exchange for a "love offering." Stands were set up in the temple's foyer to sell full-color, autographed pictures of Jones and other items to protect buyers from harm.[31]

Others follow this pattern today. With professional, ghost-written letters, one televangelist pleads for money and offers gimmicks—prayer cloths, prayer cords, arrows to aim at needs, tracings of his hand, water from the "Jordan River," "holy anointing" oil—with supernatural power to bring about the "miracles" his followers need.

## Pressure

Admittedly, Jim Jones is an extreme example of greed. But present-day aberrant leaders also are exerting undue pressure to give simply by sending frequent letters with personalized addresses.

Others push and shove. In a recent mailing, a televangelist included a yellow envelope with these words in bold, black letters: "*Do not open* this envelope until you have read my letter and returned your prayer requests to me" (along with money, of course). Inside was a supposedly handwritten note which said in part:

> My Dear Friend, From the moment I began to write this letter, I have felt such a powerful anointing flowing into my being for miracles . . . . This is truly a prophetic letter sent from God through me to you! 2 Chronicles 20:20b states, "Believe his prophets, so shall ye prosper." I have delivered unto you that which God has given me to say. *Believe it!! receive it!! and act on it!! in faith.*

On the donation coupon, it says, "I am going to *sow a seed* of faith for my harvest of Blessings of the Earth. I hereby set my faith in agreement with yours . . . as I honor God first with this gift and believe for a double portion blessing of earthly needs," followed by various amounts, beginning with one hundred dollars.[32]

## Deceit

When an aberrant leader cannot get all the money he wants through pressure, he often resorts to deceitful means.

The pastor of a church in a Seattle suburb decided to move the core of his church to Florida in the late 1970s. To finance the move, he urged his young followers to sell their homes, cars, and furniture. He would sell the church building. They would put all their money in one "pot" like the early church did in Acts—share and share alike.

While still in the Seattle area, the pastor formed a new construction company with a board of Christian businessmen to back him. The board members, however, had no idea that he was moving to Florida with his congregation, several of whom began working for the new company. When he later left town, his company folded. The newly formed board was left to pick up the pieces of his bankruptcy.

Meanwhile, the small congregation began their trek to Florida with one of the elders in charge. The pastor stayed to close the sale of their church building. The money from the sale, however, never reached the community pot. Former members say no one knows where it went, but they have heard since that the leader has bank accounts in Seattle, New York, San Diego, Florida, and possibly Switzerland.

When "the fathering apostle," as the leader called himself, finally arrived on the scene in his Cadillac, he looked around at the old house where his followers lived in crowded conditions. Then he bought a spacious air-conditioned house for himself and his family, just in time for the hot, humid summer.

After the congregation had lived in community for several months, the leader called a special meeting. He talked at length about "unity in the Spirit" and being part of God's family. Then he got down to the core of his speech: Anyone who left the group could not take the money he or she had contributed.

Still in the honeymoon stage of living together, his followers thought it unlikely they would ever want to leave "the body of Christ." So all of them signed a statement saying that they would not take any money they had put into group funds, nor would they press to get it back.

Later, when the authoritarian control became unbearable in the commune, disillusioned members regretted signing that statement. Those who finally left went out penniless.[33]

As Diane Sawyer pointed out, some televangelists also use deceit to get the money they want. The response from pleas of one man was overwhelming—truckloads of letters, prayer requests, returned gimmicks, and eighty million dollars a year. As we have said, the envelopes go unopened to his bank, where employees remove money and throw prayer requests and gimmicks into the garbage.[34]

He was not alone in using deceit to bilk his followers. In the summer of 1992, another televangelist told his viewers that his home burned to the ground, destroying almost everything he and his family had. For a gift of thirty dollars, his viewers could have a tape: "How [the leader] Applied Lessons to His Own Life After Fire Destroyed His Home."

He told Sawyer in an interview, "We lost our furniture. We lost our home. And we lost most of our clothes."

"Everything you had?"

"Yes."

Not quite everything, she discovered. His house in Tulsa, Oklahoma, did burn, "an insured house [he] had been trying to sell without luck for two years," Sawyer said. "But," she added, he "didn't lose *this* house—a 5-acre estate outside Dallas, where he's been living for the past six years." The camera showed the Dallas house "filled with furniture, books, family photos." His maid and nanny were still working there.[35]

*Threats*

In 1987, a televangelist told his donors in appeal letters and on television that unless he raised a total of eight million above regular ministry expenses by the end of March, he would die.[36]

Some say that even if he were sincere, his appeals were "a type of emotional blackmail." As writer Randy Frame says:

[He] often implies that a supporter must send him money in order to receive a blessing. In his latest fundraising letter, for example, he wrote:

"I know in my spirit if you neglect going into this agreement with the anointed prophet who is offering it to you, then what I can do to help you get your miracles will soon be over."[37]

Some followers saw this as a threat. According to current ratings, 63 percent of his audience is fifty years old or older and may be more easily swayed by his warnings.[38] Jack Sims, minister and financial consultant to churches and religious organizations, claims that studies show that the average donor to this man's ministry is "a 55-year-old, rural, Southern woman with a low income and limited education."[39]

By early February 1987, he had received over one hundred thousand letters of response from his partners. Only six were negative.[40] The money apparently did come in by March 31, thanks in large part to a dog-track owner who contributed $1.3 million.[41]

*Results of Greed and Fraud*

Diane Sawyer on ABC's *PrimeTime Live* investigation in 1992 pulled off the masks of the three prominent televangelists featured. What has happened to them since?

The first one, whose "sanctified" trinkets and prayer requests returned from viewers were dumped in the trash, is off the air. His church of five thousand members dwindled to 320. He sold his Florida seaside mansion and his twelve-thousand-foot "parsonage" in Dallas, Texas. He laid off 70 percent of his employees and divorced his wife. As if that were not enough, he has been the recipient of ten lawsuits and numerous government investigations.[42]

The second televangelist, who majored in healing, has gone off the air, at least as of this writing. He is trying to recoup his losses, however, by direct-mail appeals. For instance, he offers neckties which he wore "while the anointing of the Holy Ghost" was on him—for a ninety-one dollars each donation. One such tie healed a man in intensive care, and another helped a man get the best job of his life, the televangelist says.[43]

The third popular televangelist claimed that his family just had the clothes on their backs after their home burned; then Diane Sawyer showed photos of his other mansion full of valuables. After the exposé, his ministry was crippled. Donations dried up, churches canceled his speaking engagements, and he found himself $800,000 in debt. He left Tulsa, Oklahoma, and took the pastorate of a church in La Mesa, California. Unrepentant, he wrote his supporters that *PrimeTime* aired "lies and distortions" about him and his ministry that they "spoon-fed to an unsuspecting American public."

Amazingly, two prominent Christian leaders have given him their blessing. In his next appeal letter, the televangelist wrote, "Falsely accused, fully exonerated." His urged his supporters to get behind "Operation Goliath," his debt-reduction campaign and to give "an amount that seems impossible."[44]

In contrast, godly leaders are faithful in financial matters. George Müller (1805-1898) of Bristol, England, was one of these. As a young person, however, he seemed an unlikely candidate. He began systematically stealing money from his father at the age of ten, a practice he kept up for years. When in high school, he spent all his money, then pretended he had been robbed. Fellow students and teachers collected money to cover his "losses."

However, after his conversion, Müller recognized greed and stealing as sin and confessed them as such. He grew spiritually through Bible study, prayer, and fellowship with believers. Later, as a young pastor, he determined "to receive no fixed salary for any service rendered to God's people," according to his biographer, A. T. Pierson.[45]

Still later, Müller felt he needed to deal with his natural tendency of covetousness even further. So he decided not to ask others for help, even indirectly, by stating his needs.

As Müller dealt severely with his besetting sin of greed, God entrusted him with millions of pounds for his work. Müller meticulously accounted for every penny. By 1870, he housed and fed two thousand orphans in large dormitories near Bristol. In addition, he supported 189 missionaries overseas, had one hundred elementary schools with nine thousand students, and distributed four million tracts and tens of thousands of Bibles. For all this, he looked to God alone for funds and never appealed to people.

Müller himself offers an example in sacrificial giving. Although he received thousands for his work, he kept only what was absolutely necessary for his needs and put the rest into the ministry. He laid up treasure in heaven, not on earth.

Müller's example of looking only to God for supplies influenced many others to do the same. One was missionary Hudson Taylor, founder of the China Inland Mission. He followed Müller's pattern of "moving men through God by prayer alone."

## What God Says About Greed and Fraud

1. *God says we are all greedy by nature.* Jeremiah the prophet, for instance, grieves over this sin among leaders and laypeople alike: "From the least to the greatest, all are greedy for gain; prophets and priests alike, all practice deceit" (Jer. 6:13).

2. *God says greedy teachers will enter the church from without.* Jesus warned about thieves creeping in among the flock of God: "I tell you the truth, the man who does not enter the sheep pen by the gate, but climbs in some other way, is a thief and a robber. . . . The thief comes only to steal and kill

and destroy . . . . The man runs away [in time of danger] because he is a hired hand and cares nothing for the sheep" (John 10:1,10,13).

Such a leader, Jesus implies, is a thief whose purpose is to steal from the sheep. He is a hired hand; he's in the religion business for money. He doesn't care about the sheep.

This ties in with what the prophet Ezekiel said about selfish shepherds over God's flock: "Woe to the shepherds of Israel who only take care of themselves! Should not shepherds take care of the flock? You eat the curds, clothe yourselves with the wool and slaughter the choice animals, but you do not take care of the flock" (Ezek. 34:2–3).

In his farewell to the Ephesian elders, the apostle Paul urged them to "keep watch" over themselves and "all the flock of which the Holy Spirit" had made them overseers. In fact, he commanded them to be on their guard. "Remember," he said, "that for three years I never stopped warning each of you night and day with tears" (Acts 20:28, 31).

Of what did Paul warn these elders? Read his words carefully: "I know that after I leave, savage wolves will come in among you and will not spare the flock" (v. 29).

In this passage, Paul warned of danger to the flock from without. Fierce wolves, he said, would creep stealthily into the fold under cover of darkness and pounce on the sheep, not sparing any. He implied that the sheep would not be prepared for this danger, but would be careless, feeling content and secure in the company of their friends. These wolves would be out for their own gain, intent on feasting off the fat sheep.

*3. God says that greedy teachers will arise from within the church.* The second warning Paul gave was danger to the flock from within: "Even from your own number men will arise and distort the truth in order to draw away disciples after them" (Acts 20:30).

In the course of time, he said, false teachers and prophets would arise from within the ranks of the church. They would draw disciples to themselves by distorting and misinterpreting Scripture. No doubt these men would be articulate and make what they said sound right, convincing many. What they would teach, however, would be the opposite of what the apostles taught. Yet it would sound so good that many would be deceived.

Paul also warned Timothy about false teachers "who think that godliness is a means to financial gain" (1 Tim. 6:5).

*4. God says that such leaders defraud Christians.* The apostle Peter warned: "In their greed these teachers will exploit you with stories they have made up" (2 Pet. 2:3).

In the Greek language, the word *greed* means "fraudulency, extortion, eager for gain, defrauding." The word *exploit* means "to travel in a country as a pedlar, to trade and make gain." Such leaders financially exploit their victims, all too often the widowed or elderly.

*5. God says that greed ends in ruin and destruction.* Paul warns believers and leaders alike of the dangers of covetousness: "People who want to get rich fall into temptation and a trap and into many foolish and harmful desires that plunge men into ruin and destruction. For the love of money is a root of all kinds of evil. Some people, eager for money, have wandered from the faith and pierced themselves with many griefs" (1 Tim. 6:9–10).

God says through the prophet Ezekiel: "I will remove them from tending the flock so that the shepherds can no longer feed themselves. I will rescue my flock from their mouths, and it will no longer be food for them" (Ezek. 34:10).

In contrast, Paul reminds the Ephesian elders that he has not been covetous: "I have not coveted anyone's silver or gold or clothing. You yourselves know that these hands of mine have supplied my own needs and the needs of my companions. In everything I did, I showed you that by this kind of hard work we must help the weak, remembering the words the Lord Jesus himself said: 'It is more blessed to give than to receive'" (Acts 20:33–35).

As Christians, we need to be responsible stewards of our money. We should give generously to our churches and their outreach programs, since we are familiar with their spending practices.

For any other program or organization, we need to ask ourselves these important questions before giving:

1. Is the need real, or is the plea a ploy to get us to give?

2. Are we sure this is what God wants us to do, or are we responding to an emotional appeal?

3. Is the appeal for money done in a manipulative manner? Are there either threats or promises of great blessing?

4. Is the group honest and spending money wisely? Does

it furnish a financial statement upon request? Is it a member of the Evangelical Council for Financial Accountability (ECFA)?

## Questions
1. How does an aberrant leader control his people's giving?
2. What promises does he make his followers?
3. What means does he use to get money?
4. What questions should we ask ourselves before giving to organizations other than our churches?

# Chapter 7

# Immorality

Sexual sins take a personal toll on the victim,
leaving the person in bondage,
increasingly less satisfied,
and on a downward spiral
which only results in greater tragedy.
—Charles R. Swindoll[1]

*Agnes*
Deep in the forests of southern Mexico, we young people
were at Jungle Training Camp conducted by Wycliffe Bible
Translators. As a single girl at "advance base," my
companions and I were learning skills we might need later
in primitive locations.

One skill was paddling dugout canoes. These were not
your usual Western-style aluminum or fiberglass canoes. The
Mexican Indians had dug them out of solid tree trunks, so
they were heavy with thick sides.

One day our leaders took thirteen of us in four canoes on
a two-day trip. It was the thrill of a lifetime to shoot the rapids
downstream.

But going upstream the next day was a different story. We
paddled when we could, then got out and pulled our canoes
through thirty rapids.

Four of us were paddling through a deep, rough section
when we shipped water until the canoe sank. We piled out
and started swimming.

To my terror, I found myself separated from my companions and swept into a circle on the edge of a whirlpool. Even though I was a good swimmer, an irresistible force like an elevator plummeted me downward. I clawed my way to the top and gasped for air before being sucked down again. When this happened the third time, I thought my lungs would burst. I knew I was drowning.

*God, help!* I silently screamed under water.

Suddenly, like the whale expelling Jonah, I was propelled to the top and out of the vortex. I struggled toward the beach through the rushing water and waved my arm.

Two fellows on shore saw my signal, swam out to me, and pulled me on dry land.

My experience reminds me of a leader getting caught in immorality. An affair starts out innocently enough, he thinks, but in time it sucks him into the "downward spiral" of sexual sin. Too late, he finds that immorality destroys his ministry, his personal freedoms, and his family relationships.

## Immorality Destroys Ministries

A Louisiana-based televangelist was a catalyst in the downfall of a North Carolina televangelist. He charged that the talk-show host committed adultery with a former church secretary.

The young secretary admitted her involvement and that she had accepted a settlement from the televangelist's lawyers totaling $265,000. She claimed she had been "lured to a hotel, drugged, and forcibly seduced." He, on the other hand, asserted that he was the unsuspecting victim of a temptress who "knew all the tricks of the trade."[2]

According to her, she was twenty-one when another evangelist encouraged her to fly to Florida to meet the popular televangelist, whom she idolized. At a hotel, she said, she was given drugged wine and forced to give him a back rub. She resisted his advances, but was unable to fight him off. Afterwards, she felt like "a piece of hamburger thrown into the street."

After brooding about her encounter for years, she finally contacted his aide in 1984. He told her to forget it, but a friend of hers in California drew up a lawsuit. The televangelist's lawyers promised to pay $115,000 immediately, $20,000 to her and the rest for fees. In addition, they put $150,000 in trust. She would receive $800 to $1,000 a month and all the principal—if she kept quiet for twenty years.

Someone on the talk show staff gave the story to the *Charlotte Observer.* Someone else urged his denomination to act. The result? He resigned.[3]

The Louisiana-based televangelist defended his accusations as hating sin and loving the sinner, as cutting cancer out of the body of Christ. On national TV, he decried, "I'm ashamed; I'm embarrassed. The Gospel of Jesus Christ has never sunk to such a level as it has today."[4]

The irony of it all is that this second televangelist was later accused of sexual indiscretion himself. He was photographed going into a motel with a prostitute. On Sunday, February 20, 1988, he confessed with tears before his crowded church that he had sinned against God, his wife, his family, and his congregation. He asked all to forgive him.[5]

Instead of coming under the discipline of his denomination, however, he left it in 1988 to continue his church and TV ministries on his own.

Another incident further besmirched the evangelist's name on October 12, 1991. In California for meetings, he picked up a streetwalker "for sex. That's why he stopped me," she explained. "That's what I do. I'm a prostitute," she told KNBC-TV in Los Angeles.

Police discovered the pair when they cited him for driving an unregistered 1989 Jaguar, for driving on the wrong side of the road, and for not wearing a seat belt.

When the evangelist saw a police car behind him, the prostitute said, he "became agitated, swerving his car as he tried to hide pornographic magazines."[6]

The evangelist refused to talk about the incident. "The Lord told me it's flat none of your business," he told his congregation when he got home.[7]

But some felt it was their business. Several of his top officials resigned. Others were fired. A number of television stations canceled their contracts with his program.[8]

His ministry had brought in $150 million annually, reaching eight million viewers weekly in the U.S. and millions more in 145 countries. But by 1991, he was $4.5 million in the red and faced with numerous expensive lawsuits. Enrollment at his $100 million Bible college plummeted. An unfinished dormitory sits idle with empty window frames and weeds choking its doors.[9]

The evangelist and his once-prosperous TV empire were sucked into a downward spiral.

## Immorality Destroys Personal Freedoms

A community church located on sixty-eight forested acres of Vashon Island in Puget Sound, Washington, was a religious commune of friendly people who lived in spacious new homes. They were led by a husky, six-foot-four pastor and a woman copastor.

In July of 1977, the pastor, his wife, and a few church friends moved from northern Illinois to western Washington to save heating costs and to obtain land where they could live close to one another. Other believers joined them as they sold homes and businesses in Illinois, making a total of more than sixty people in the commune. At first they lived in tents while building their comfortable homes.[10]

The leader formerly pastored a denominational church in Ingleside, Illinois, a small town near the Wisconsin border. In 1977, church officials charged him with "unministerial behavior" and forced him to relinquish his pastorate, according to his former district superintendent in the northern Illinois conference. His investigation revealed that this pastor held private sexually oriented "therapy" sessions.[11]

The pastor "withdrew from the church to avoid a [heresy] trial," the district superintendent said. "He did great injury to a church here. He represents a personally destructive force that prevents those in his group from developing normally. He is the dictator; he is the dominator of the whole group."[12]

In 1983, former members of the church on Vashon Island brought a lawsuit against the leader and his wife for forcing men and women to attend sexual "therapy" sessions, to shower together, and to share toilet facilities. Such things were supposed to "help people shed sexual hangups and dissolve feelings of one another as sex objects." They further claimed that the leader "taught the community to lie and to lie convincingly" regarding such activities.[13]

Debby, an attractive young woman, charged the pastor with misconduct when she was seventeen years old. In 1980, he forced her to live aboard his boat for many months, where he sexually abused her. He punished her if she resisted.

"It seemed to me," Debby said, "that [his] whole outlook was sex. I felt really trapped. I knew in my heart and my head that what they [the leader and his wife] were doing wasn't right. I felt like I was hanging onto something in my life, and if I let go, I'd be a goner."[14]

The pastor denied the charges brought against him, his wife, and his church and accused the plaintiffs of wrong motives. "They have taken something that was very innocent and very beautiful and twisted it into something very nasty," the leader told reporter John Hessburg. "I will say right now before God my creator, I have not touched another human being sexually, except my wife, since 1943 . . . . I'm a man of high integrity. I'm totally committed to Christ." They are "telling lies to hurt us," he claimed.[15]

Former member Shirley said of this leader, "I believe [he] has completely departed from the Christian religion. I think that this is satanic; this is not of God. It destroys people's self-will, their initiative." She believes the leader makes his followers psychological slaves.[16]

They've lost their personal freedoms in the whirlpool of deviant sexual behavior.

## Immorality Destroys Family Relationships
The founder and pastor of a community church in Washington led his three-thousand followers into wholesale adultery.

In the spring of 1985, he preached a series of sermons on "Spiritual and Soulical Relationships." This pastor "decreed that the highest form of spiritual realization could be found by dancing at church services with someone else's spouse . . . . Dancing with one's 'connection' opened up the possibility of pure spiritual love," he said.[17]

Before this, members of the chapel often danced solo during services. Now they chose partners other than their spouses and danced together, "holding hands, hugging, embracing, and kissing" each other. When an individual found the "right" person, he became "spiritually connected" with her. "Connected" couples could then "express the love of Christ and the unity of His church by putting their spirits together."[18]

One investigator who attended services at the chapel, described the scene: "They're hugging, caressing and dancing in the pews, in the hallways and in rooms set aside just for dancing." Some "connected" couples danced more privately in Room E-250 where a few were seen lying together. According to church bulletins, dancing services occurred every night. Some were closed to the public.

In his sermons, the pastor defined a "soulical connection" as "the physical relationship between husband and wife." A "spiritual connection," on the other hand, "is an experience of Christ realized in a loving dance with someone other than a spouse."[19]

When the leader asked for a show of hands of those whose marriages had been healed or improved by spiritual connections, most members raised their hands, according to one observer.

However, the results have not been good. The teaching of "spiritual connections" has resulted in defection, adultery, child abuse, and broken marriages. The pastor's own marriage has dissolved, and his wife and children have left.

Some members have had nervous breakdowns or committed suicide, even murder. Janet, a young wife and mother and a member of the church, drove to Portland, Oregon, checked into the Ramada Inn, and drowned her five-year-old daughter in the bathtub. The mother told investigators that she did it to save her daughter's soul. Convinced that both she and her daughter were demon-possessed, she felt her little girl's salvation was assured if she died before the age of accountability.

Previously, this attractive thirty-five-year-old housewife had a nervous breakdown after becoming involved with a "spiritual connection," a man other than her husband. "He fell in love with her, and she knew it was improper," says a friend. "She didn't know how to reconcile her feelings."[20]

This teaching also resulted in the split of the church. On March 4, 1988, the elders of the chapel and Bible school fired the founding pastor. They ousted him because he "failed to respond to elders' restrictions imposed on him for alleged sexual misconduct," a church spokesman said. They charged him with "sexual sin of substantial magnitude" with women in the congregation.[21]

This action, however, "won't be enough to stop the adultery and child abuse," a former administrative staff member charged. The church "has become a sex cult and will remain a sex cult unless its teachings and its leadership are completely changed."

"Spiritual connections" between church members and elders continue. "There is nothing spiritual about these relationships," he said. He describes them as "church-sanctioned affairs that have broken up marriages, disrupted families, caused suicides and suicide attempts, and traumatized children."

He added, "The tragedy is these kids have a warped concept of marriage and life that they're going to have for years and years."

"Chapel members have been frightened with warnings that leaving the church will plunge them into sin or alcoholism or cause them to go to hell," the former staff member said. "It simply isn't true." He has been able to straighten out his life after leaving. "There is life after [being in the chapel]," he said. "And it's very good."[22]

In a hearing on March 11, 1988, a King County Superior Court judge ordered that the leader be reinstated as pastor. Following this, about four hundred of his faithful rallied around him in the main sanctuary for worship services. However, the elders and their supporters met in the church's Bible-college building.[23]

Former members are critical of the teaching and practice of "spiritual connections." An ordained Pentecostal minister who left wrote the congregation, criticizing the pastor's "perversion of the pure Word of God. Licentious worship leading inevitably to 'free love' has been around a long time," he wrote. "Marriages are ruined, children observing the hypocrisy are lost, and the name of Jesus is brought into reproach."

A former Assembly of God minister and the chapel's "prophet" and his wife, superintendent of their elementary school, left in March of 1986. In a letter to the pastor, they said, "We cannot agree with the teaching of the intimate dance and relationships with other people's mates. We feel it is unscriptural."

Former member Marjorie described her experiences with "spiritual connections":

[The pastor's wife] described a vision she had. She saw God's white, holy room of love. Some had entered in [by having spiritual connections], but others were hanging around the outside of the door. They were going to be swept away if they didn't get involved with what God was doing with spiritual connections. I was scared. I wanted to find a connection and be perfected in God . . . .

One man wanted to be my connection. He was married. His wife had fallen in love with her connection and eventually left with him. . . . One day he said he had another connection. He wasn't going to spend time with me anymore because I was too "soulical" and dependent on him. By then, all my friends had connections and didn't have time to do things with me anymore. I felt really abandoned. Hurt. Scared. I felt I wasn't going to make it into the white, holy room of God's love. I wasn't going to be the "perfected bride" [of Christ] because I had lost my connection. I became almost hysterical. One night another man asked me to dance with him. He was very sweet, gentle, and seemed more stable than the others I had met. So I felt I could trust him. Looking back, I feel I was very vulnerable. We spent a lot of time together, sharing, praying, and dancing. His wife became so jealous, she would hardly speak to me. Eventually we had an affair. He and his wife later left the church, and I was abandoned again.[24]

The pastor's older brother, a minister in Boise, Idaho, says, "I love my brother. I've tried to warn him, but he doesn't take heed. I'm praying that God will recover him from this deep deception of Satan."[25]

The relationships of the chapel families have been lost in the whirlpool of immorality.

Another case in point is a former commune in western Washington. The whole operation was swathed in secrecy. Visitors were not welcome. Two German shepherd dogs guarded the entrance.

The reason became clear in 1979–1980 when the leader was charged and convicted of third-degree statutory rape of a fifteen-year-old girl and of indecently touching a twelve-year-old girl. Several other young women testified during the long trial about years of sexual contact with him.[26]

Teenagers Carol and Beth, daughters of group members, moved in with the leader and his wife. Supposedly the couple would help the girls grow spiritually. Instead, the leader took them to pornographic films, then both to bed with him, according to Peggy, Carol's mother. Beth finally left the group, but Carol is still there and refuses to come home.

One evening another member's daughter, seventeen-year-old Donna, confessed to Peggy that the leader had forced her to have sex with him once a week since she was fourteen years old. After leaving the group, an adult member told Peggy that she and most of the other women had had their turn with the leader also.

Peggy is heartbroken about her daughter Carol. "I try to talk to her [by phone], but he's done something with the girls' minds and bodies. They don't have any respect for their bodies anymore. He has ruined them."[27]

And he has ruined the family relationships of his followers.

David Koresh, leader of the Branch Davidians, got sucked into the whirlpool of immorality also.

According to former member David Bunds, Koresh supposedly had a divine revelation in 1986 that affected the group's whole attitude toward marriage. He was to practice polygamy to start the "house of David," so he took the single girls of the commune as his "wives."

By 1989, Bunds says, Koresh decided to add the married women to his harem. After all, King Solomon had "threescore queens, and fourscore concubines, and virgins without number" (Song of Sol. 6:8 KJV). The marriages of these women "became null and void, and they became joined to Koresh" alone. They could no longer have sex with their husbands or anyone else.

"He was considered married to my sister and later to my mother," Bunds says. "He was also married to sisters, that is, to his first wife and later to her younger sister."[28]

Koresh's propensity for deviant sexual behavior dates back to 1981 when he impregnated the fifteen-year-old minister's daughter of the Seventh-Day Adventist Church in Tyler, Texas. That act resulted in his being disfellowshiped from the church and joining the Branch Davidians.[29]

He soon had an ongoing affair with Lois Roden, then in

her sixties and leader of the commune after the death of her husband Benjamin.[30]

Koresh even included girls as young as ten or eleven years old in his deviant scheme. He gave them plastic stars of David indicating that they had "the light" and "were ready to have sex" with him.[31]

After all, as "David," he needed to produce a great many children/followers for his kingdom reign in Jerusalem.

In the process, he destroyed the family relationships of his entire commune before they went up in flames.

## What God Says About Immorality

1. *Jesus said that immorality begins in the mind:* "I tell you that anyone who looks at a woman lustfully has already committed adultery with her in his heart" (Matt. 5:28). "For out of the heart come evil thoughts, murder, adultery, sexual immorality" (Matt. 15:19).

After resounding victories in Ammonite-Syrian campaigns, King David relaxed in his palace in Jerusalem. The Ammonites attacked again, but he sent commander Joab and the Israeli army to quell them. He was too tired; they'd have to get along without him.

One evening David awoke from a nap and walked around the roof of the palace surveying his domain. Suddenly he stopped pacing. His eyes fastened on a woman bathing on a nearby roof—and she was the most beautiful he had ever seen. His mind wandered. As Jesus said, he looked at her "lustfully" and "committed adultery with her in his heart."

Instead of refusing to dwell on the temptation, he yielded to it. He sent messengers to bring Bathsheba, the wife of the soldier Uriah, to his bedchamber (2 Sam. 11:1–5).

2. *God says to resist temptation and keep our bodies pure:* "The body is not meant for sexual immorality, but for the Lord. . . . Do you not know that your bodies are members of Christ himself? Shall I then take the members of Christ and unite them with a prostitute? Never! Do you not know that he who unites himself with a prostitute is one with her in body? For it is said, 'The two will become one flesh'" (1 Cor. 6:13, 15–16).

"Among you there must not be even a hint of sexual immorality, or of any kind of impurity, or of greed, because these are improper for God's holy people" (Eph. 5:3).

God tells us what to do with this sin: "Put to death . . .

whatever belongs to your earthly nature: sexual immorality, impurity, lust, evil desires and greed" (Col. 3:5).

Joseph is a shining example of one who resisted temptation. Potiphar, captain of the Egyptian Pharaoh's guard, put the responsible Israeli slave in charge of his entire estate. But Potiphar's wife, enamored with Joseph's handsome physique, lusted after him. Day after day she flaunted herself before him and pled with him to have an affair with her.

Lonely and homesick, Joseph could have reasoned that no one would ever know. He had worked so hard, he deserved this reward. Instead, he said, "How could I do such a wicked thing and sin against God?"

One day when they were alone in the house, she grabbed hold of him. "Come to bed with me!" she pleaded.

"No!" he said. He struggled out of his cloak and ran.

This decision was costly. It not only meant the loss of his good reputation and job, but his angry master had him thrown into prison. Eventually God rewarded his faithfulness by making him prime minister of Egypt and the means of saving his people from starvation (see Gen. 39:1–23; 41:39–43).

*3. God warns of immoral teachers within the church:* "With eyes full of adultery, they never stop sinning; they seduce the unstable" (2 Pet. 2:14).

"We need to understand the insidiousness of sexual misconduct when it is combined with spiritual deception," says counselor Linda Medill Hall. "After his followers have elevated a spiritual leader to a place of power as an 'oracle of God,' they find it difficult to question his actions. All he does—right or wrong—is cloaked in an aura of spirituality. To refuse his sexual advances is to refuse God, he says. To cooperate with him is to cooperate with God.

"Thus the normal alarm bells which go off inside a person's mind when she is sexually violated are muffled," Hall continues. "The desire to please God or the fear of displeasing him overpowers inner warnings. So seduction conducted with spiritual overtones is extremely disorienting and is a particularly evil use of power."[32]

Such a leader does not develop honest, open relationships with peers. One man who resigned from the presidency of an international Christian fellowship because of adultery, concluded: "I now realize I was lacking in mutual accountability through personal relationships. We need friendships where one man regularly looks another man in the eye and asks hard questions about our moral life, our lust, our ambitions, our ego."[33]

*4. God warns of severe judgment on immorality:* "Because of these [sins], the wrath of God is coming" (Col. 3:6). Moreover he says: "For of this you can be sure: No immoral, impure or greedy person . . . has any inheritance in the kingdom of Christ and of God.

"Let no one deceive you with empty words, for because of such things God's wrath comes on those who are disobedient. Therefore do not be partners with them" (Eph. 5:6–7).

Even though a true believer does not lose his salvation by committing adultery, he still bears the punishment for his sin.

King David, for instance, when confronted by the prophet Nathan, repented and asked God's forgiveness for both adultery and the murder of Bathsheba's husband.

God forgave him, but said he would forever bear the consequences: "Now, therefore, the sword will never depart from your house, because you despised me and took the wife of Uriah the Hittite to be your own . . . . Out of your own household I am going to bring calamity upon you" (2 Sam. 12:10–11).

Results? The first son of his union with Bathsheba died. David's son Amnon raped his stepsister Tamar. His son Absalom rebelled and almost succeeded in taking the kingdom.

No one can avoid the consequences. Immorality destroys ministries, personal freedoms, and family relationships.

And it sucks its victims into a "downward spiral" of destruction.

## Questions
1. Describe how immorality destroys ministries.
2. How does it destroy personal freedoms?
3. What does immorality do to family relationships? Describe. What effect does it have on children?
4. How can sexual sins lead to murder?

5. Where does immorality begin?
6. How can followers justify committing sexual sins with their leader?
7. How does God judge immorality?
8. How can small accountability groups of peers help solve the problem of immorality?

# Chapter 8

# Enslaving Authoritarian Structure

Of all plagues with which mankind are cursed,
Ecclesiastic tyranny's the worst.
—Daniel Defoe

The United States Navy is known for one of its basic rules—submission to authority. And rightly so.

However, in the event of "extraordinary circumstances," a subordinate may put an officer under arrest or on the sick list and take command.

Such an "extraordinary circumstance" alledgedly took place in the South Pacific during World War II. In December of 1944, the US Navy's mighty Third Fleet steamed toward the Philippines to support General Douglas MacArthur's invasion.

On December 18, an unexpected typhoon, with winds up to ninety-three knots, approached the fleet from the rear. Seventy-foot waves crashed over the vessels, washing men overboard, tearing planes loose from carrier decks, and plunging them into the raging sea.

The destroyers—smaller, low on fuel, and top-heavy—took the worst beating. Winds pushed their stacks horizontally. Water poured through ventilators, killing their power and setting them adrift. Three destroyers capsized, the *Spence*, the *Hull*, and the *Monaghan*. Twenty-eight other ships were heavily damaged, two hundred planes were wrecked, and 790 American lives were lost in the storm.[1]

In his historical novel *The Caine Mutiny,* author Herman Wouk tells what may have happened during this typhoon aboard the fictional minesweeper *Caine.* The captain, Lieutenant Commander Queeg, slavishly kept in formation on the prescribed course. As the storm mounted in fury, his second in command, Steve Maryk, shouted, "Sir, we can't ride stern to wind and save this ship!" The emotionally unbalanced captain stood with arms and legs entwined around the telegraph stand. His voice was almost a whisper. "Mr. Maryk, fleet course is 180." The executive officer saluted. "Captain, I'm sorry, sir, but you're a sick man. I am temporarily relieving you of command of this ship, under Article 184 of *Navy Regulations.*"[2] Maryk knew he could be charged with mutiny. But his turning the *Caine* around and heading into the wind saved both his ship and crew.

In the same way, we Christians must use our God-given judgment and not slavishly follow orders from someone over us.

Yet that is exactly what an aberrant Christian group wants us to do. Its very structure evidences a hunger for power. It sets up an authoritarian pyramid so it can control the personal lives of its members. The leader is at the top, of course, with a hierarchy of underlings to carry out his wishes.

David Koresh and his Branch Davidians were nightmarish examples of a leader with unlimited control. New followers were "whisked into another world" when they joined the commune where Koresh was "absolute ruler," says former member David Bunds. The leader controlled "all aspects of life in the group, down to hygiene, diet, eating times, [and] sleep."

What if one resisted or refused to obey? "The punishments for disobedience progressed as time went on," says Bunds. "At first, you might be chastised verbally, later on, denied a meal or excluded from a study that would reveal some special light. He would make you feel bad that you didn't get to hear it. Later he would have one of his bigger men beat you up a bit with a stick or something. This happened to male members.

"Children also were severely punished," says Bunds.

Koresh believed in "punishment with a paddle on the behind." Sometimes children were "spanked for very long periods of time to the point of blood." In fact, Koresh commanded Bunds' sister to paddle her son until "he was actually bleeding."[3]

This type of domination occurs not only in actual cults. Critics today express concern about evangelical Christians flocking to sects "dominated by leaders who exercise virtually unlimited control over members' lives and thoughts. . . . What sets the new groups apart from the older sects and mainstream churches . . . is the great degree of power held by the leaders."[4]

Although these groups hold to the basic tenets of the evangelical Christian faith, for the most part, they have formed authoritarian structures to keep tight control over their followers.

In the 1970s and 1980s, the shepherding movement was considered by some as "the fastest growing element within fundamentalist Christianity." It is one of the leading proponents of authoritarianism.

In a genuine effort to help new believers, five ministers in Florida joined forces. They set up a pyramid structure with themselves on top and a hierarchy of "shepherds" or "pastors" under them who in turn cared for thousands of disciples. Their teaching spread worldwide through seminars, conferences, books, tapes, and a magazine. An example of its hierarchical structure is depicted on the chart *The Shepherding Pyramid* on the next page.

## Areas of Control

An aberrant authoritarian group seeks not only to control its members' beliefs, but also their decisions and practices. To make this control binding, members must submit to the leadership, either vocally or in writing, in all areas of life.

### Control of Time

In an authoritarian setting, group activities occupy members' free time. Shepherding leaders require them to attend home meetings and church services regularly.

Karen, a woman in her early twenties, joined a "community" for young people sponsored by our shepherding church. When she moved in, she was excited

---

**International Leaders**
Shepherd the bishops

**Bishops**
Oversee church networks
Shepherded by international leaders

**Presiding Elders**
Pastor individual churches
Shepherded by bishops

**Elders**
Several serve in each church
Shepherded by presiding elders

**Home-Meeting Leaders or "Pastors"**
Shepherd cell groups
Shepherded by elders

**Men Members**
Members of home groups and churches
Shepherded by home-meeting leaders or "pastors"

**Women Members**
Married women shepherded by husbands
Single women shepherded by
home-meeting leaders or pastors

---

## The Shepherding Pyramid

about the possibilities for spiritual growth in a close-knit fellowship.

Although Karen was a committed Christian, she soon found "the control unreal." Later she told us, "Home meetings, information meetings, church attendance, work parties, and family nights were all mandatory. We were expected to be there. If we weren't, the leader checked up on us. Even feeling tired or sick were no excuses." Her time was not her own.

In their book *Damaged Disciples*, former shepherding-movement members Ron and Vicki Burks agree. Their group expected men to build and maintain leaders' houses. "Such work took every evening away from their families for months," they say.[5]

Married women spent so much time cleaning and cooking for their leaders' wives that they didn't have time to keep up with their own work.

The group expected single girls to babysit and do housework for leaders and married couples—all for free, of course. "Frequently," say the Burks, "this meant that they missed church meetings or social events so married couples could attend."[6]

Losing their own free time, members couldn't possibly think for themselves.

### Control of Large Investments

Charles and Rebekah, a retired couple in our shepherding church, wished to sell their house. Dan and Debbie, also from our church, came to look at it.

"We'd like to buy it," they said. "But first our home leader will have to check it out."

A few days later, Dan and Debbie returned with their shepherd, a young man in his early twenties. He inspected the house, then said, "Looks good to me. Go ahead with the deal."

"All of life's decisions were to be checked out with one's pastor, even the most personal ones," say Ron and Vicki Burks. "Decisions about major purchases and investments were always submitted to one's pastor," such as homes and cars. A leader could even advise couples how to decorate their houses or what furniture to buy.[7]

Any investment was directly or indirectly under their group's control.

### Control of Location

An authoritarian group often encourages followers to move near one another. In a northern California shepherding church, 150 members sold their homes, quit their jobs, and transferred to another county.

Why? One of them said, "It's important to us to form a community—a family. We want to be close to each other. We want to build a Christian community that will reflect the life of Christ. We'd all like to live on the same street, . . . but that's pretty difficult."[8]

From the time that Ron and Vicki Burks entered the shepherding movement in the early 1970s, they moved often—from Florida to Colorado to Mississippi, back to Florida, and finally to Alabama. The reason? To be close to whomever was their "pastor" then. This was the norm for others in the group, too.

This "willingness on the part of the follower to obey," the Burks say, "may mean anything from a simple commitment to follow the example of the leader, to moving either across town or across the country."[9] A shepherd can more easily control his sheep if they flock closely around him.

### Control of Marriages

An authoritarian leader helps his followers choose the right mates. In fact, they have to ask his permission to date. As Ron and Vicki Burks say: "The individual's pastor was there to help make that decision the right one. . . . Much time and effort was saved when he said that he had someone in mind and promised to talk to the other individual's pastor about it. . . . 'Wise' couples put off marriage until their pastors agreed the time was right."[10]

Couples are not only required to attend the usual pre-marital classes, but also to submit further plans to their leaders. In the experience of the Burks, a pastor "helped decide how many children a couple should have and when they should have them." He even helped choose the right names for newborns.[11]

Robert was a pastor in a campus ministry, which, critics say, has adopted shepherding teachings and practices. After his marriage to Teena, he asked if they could have a few weeks off following the wedding. His leaders refused, then sent them to a distant university to begin a new work. But the move and added workload were hard on their new marriage.

"We hardly saw each other for four months," Robert said. "But I was afraid to disagree [with the leadership]."

Result? Teena suffered an emotional breakdown, and the couple is now divorced.[12]

Sometimes a controlling group breaks up a marriage if its

leaders do not approve of it. For instance, Dennis married a young woman named Sally in a shepherding church. They had three happy weeks together. When they encountered difficulties in their physical union, Dennis consulted a staff member of the church counseling center. He shared some personal problems and confessed a sin committed before marriage.

The counselor broke confidence and told the senior pastor who became irate. He considered the young wife "like a daughter." He called her into his office and told her what he had heard. He urged her to leave her husband and move in with her home leader and his family. He also told her not to have anything more to do with Dennis—not even to speak to him on the phone.

Sally meekly obeyed.

Next, the pastor told her to come to an elders' meeting. There they laid hands on her and said in effect, "We now annul your marriage. Take back your maiden name, and live like a single girl again."

The final blow, Dennis told us, came the following Sunday when the pastor publicly excommunicated him.

Shamed, the young man drove home in a daze. The events plunged him into depression, leaving him unable to function normally for two years.

Dennis tried legal means to get his wife back, but was unsuccessful. She finally divorced him and married someone else.

Ramifications of this event have gone on for years. Dennis has tried more than once to get church leaders to meet with him if he can bring at least two witnesses.

"All I want is an apology," he told us. "I confessed my sin. Now I'd like to hear them admit they made a wrong decision and used highhanded ways."

Since the pastors refused to meet with him, Dennis sued them and the church. "I'm not interested in the money, except to pay for my expenses," he says. "But I do feel these men should be made accountable for destroying my life in a real sense and for doing similar things to others."[13]

As of this writing, the case is still pending.

## Control of Women

An interesting but painful aspect of authoritarian control

is the subjugation of women. When we were in a shepherding church, we heard one young home leader explain how we can get spiritual direction. He showed how it begins at the top with God the Father, through Jesus the Son, to and through the head pastor, the elders, the home-meeting leaders, the husbands, and finally, to the women.

"You women," he said, "should get your spiritual teaching and direction through your husbands, not on your own."

Many took this teaching to extremes. Husbands became heavy-handed in their demands. Wives became so submissive that they asked permission or direction about every detail. Instead of going to God in prayer, studying their Bibles, or using common sense, wives ran to their husbands.

The leaders put pressure on single women to come under the headship or "covering" of a shepherd, usually their home-meeting leader.

Included in this teaching were missionary women. Sarah, a mature widow, ran a rest home for missionaries in Thailand. She was partially supported by our church. While on furlough, she was anxious to share with our pastor the blessings of the past term on the field. She made an appointment and went to see him.

But the pastor was not interested in her report. "I want to know why you told the church to stop sending tapes of our services." His voice was stern.

"I have so little time to listen to them that I felt the church could use the money elsewhere." And that was true. She was busy from morning to night, seven days a week.

"And why aren't you under male headship on the field?"

"My work is independent and nondenominational," she explained. "But I do have several men missionaries on my board who advise me."

"But they're none of *our* men."

The pastor berated Sarah until she was in tears. He made it clear that she wasn't under their headship sufficiently and didn't conform to their teaching. After Sarah returned to Thailand, the church cut off her support.

Fortunately, Sarah had a good attitude about the problem. She told us in a letter, "Don't feel bad about it. The Lord is supplying my needs from other sources. He must have protected me, too, from their unbalanced teaching because I felt that something was wrong with it."

## Control of Schooling

Jack and Carol, members of a shepherding church, wanted to go to a Bible school in their city. When they talked to their pastor about it, he told them not to.

"The teaching you'll get there will be different and confusing," he said. "You'd better absorb everything you can here."

In another instance, Bob was a pastor with an authoritarian campus ministry. When he told those over him that he wished to resign so he could return to school, a leader prophesied that it was not God's will. He even said Bob and his wife would experience death and destruction if they left.[14]

## Control of Vacations

Nancy, a young career single woman, told her home leader Dan that she would like to take a week's vacation beginning the following Tuesday morning.

"Sorry," Dan replied. "You have to be at home meeting. Better make that Wednesday morning."

"Then may I be gone a week?"

"Of course not. You have to be in church Sunday morning."

In an authoritarian group, a person cannot make any major decision according to his own conscience.

Steve, a former regional director of elders with the same authoritarian campus ministry referred to earlier, gave his approval when a pastor pulled his church out of the organization.

Top leaders told him to fly to headquarters where they "accused him of being a betrayer and attempted to cast demons out of him. When one leader said they were going to take control of his life for awhile, Steve resigned."[15]

## Supposed Benefits of Control

What is the reasoning behind such control in authoritarian groups? What benefits supposedly accrue?

## Control Aids Spiritual Growth

Control enhances spiritual growth, according to leaders in the shepherding movement. Their purpose is to "provide true Christian fellowship and lead . . . members into disciplined, Bible-based lives."[16]

Those who are hungry for deeper spiritual lives are excited about being discipled by home-meeting leaders, later called "shepherds" or "personal pastors." They supposedly have an inside track to God through their elders, pastors, and on up the line to international leaders.

Tom, a young office manager, is enthusiastic about the individual help he receives from the shepherd over him. He is "a living example of following Jesus . . . . I'm going to follow this man and take on his ways and learn how to be a disciple of Jesus Christ. If all the gospel of Jesus Christ is going to do is change my Sunday schedule, then I'm not interested. I want something that is going to change my finances, my marriage, my sex life, the way I work, the way I keep my house, and the way I fix my yard."[17]

And that's exactly what a shepherd intends to do. One leader said: "If you were in my church, and you were committed to our fellowship, I would want to know a background on your family life, how you relate to women, how your wife relates to you, do you have standards of accountability with your children, where are your finances, do you pay your taxes, where are you with pornography, where are you with masturbation, where is your sex life, are you biblical in the way you approach your sexuality? These would be the sort of concerns I have. That's what it means to pastor somebody."[18]

## Control Provides Counsel

Control provides individual counseling, according to authoritarian groups. In the shepherding movement, a shepherd develops close relationships with his people by meeting as a group or individually once a week.

And what do they talk about? One home leader said: "It's really up to the person to decide what he wants to discuss. Maybe it's something with his family or a financial problem. We would talk about it, pray, and come to some decision."[19]

Many in the shepherding movement appreciate the individual attention they receive from this arrangement. They feel it is a support system that takes the place of professional counseling. One member says it develops "a closeness" and gives "that person permission in your life to help you."[20]

## Control Gives Protection

A shepherd not only stimulates spiritual growth and provides counsel, but he also protects his sheep with spiritual "covering" from the "thief and robber," Satan himself, say shepherding leaders. One pastor said: "When we say that we just follow the Lord and the Bible, that is stupid! The written Bible will not protect from error, but committed men who love us and are living out the Word certainly will."[21]

According to authoritarian groups, control also provides spiritual "covering." If sheep follow and obey their shepherd, he will protect them from error and satanic attacks. If they get out from under his covering, they will fall prey to spiritual "wolves."

"This committed relationship brings a great sense of security," Burks say. "There is the very real feeling, spiritually, of 'coming in out of the rain.'"[22]

In the process of submission and obedience, the sheep are not trained to think for themselves, but to believe as they are taught and to do as they are told.

## Basis for Authority

### Delegated Authority

Every pyramid-structured aberrant group claims that the basis for its authority comes from God himself. Leaders of the shepherding movement, for instance, teach that God wants to set up his kingdom on earth now in the hearts of men. Since Christ cannot reign in person yet, he has delegated authority to certain men who have the charisma of leadership.[23]

One of the five original shepherding leaders wrote: "[Christ] rules through delegated authority—i.e., those whom He sets in authority under Himself. Wherever His delegated authority touches our lives, He requires us to acknowledge and submit to it, just as we would to Him in person."[24]

The basis for that teaching, he writes, is in this verse, "He that receiveth whomsoever I send receiveth me; and he that receiveth me receiveth him that sent me" (John 13:20 KJV).

This establishes the principle: "Our attitude toward those whom God sets in delegated authority over us is the outward and visible expression of our attitude toward God Himself."[25]

According to one observer, a fairly new denomination believes that their group is "an outpost of the kingdom of God on earth and as such is to be governed by our reigning Lord." And how is it to be governed? Through a hierarchy of apostles, bishops, elders, and deacons. Author Bill Counts says this group teaches that "the church has an authority at least equivalent to Scripture, since the church's leaders are the final interpreters of Scripture, and must be as implicitly obeyed as God Himself."[26]

This thinking pattern is common in most authoritarian groups.

## *Rebellion—the Great Transgression*

According to shepherding and other authoritarian teaching, independence in thought and action is rebellion, which is as sinful as witchcraft. Man's great transgression is rebellion—the unwillingness to submit to authority. As one shepherding teacher explains: "When rebellion has completed its work and you are a full-grown rebel . . . self-willed . . . incorrigible . . . unchangeable—this is the great transgression—the spirit of rebellion!"[27]

## *Obedience—the Cure*

The way to overcome rebellion is to submit to and obey the commands of the one over you, say authoritarian leaders. One leader explains: "[God] says, 'Let every soul be subject unto the higher powers.' When we learn to submit to our immediate superiors, . . . suddenly we will find something breaking on the inside and our eyes will begin to open to see God's purpose and plan . . . . I dare not turn away in rebellion from that one whom God has put over me without incurring possible blindness and deafness to spiritual truth."[28]

Owen and Louise were active in a large evangelical church in California. They experienced heavy-handed tactics on the part of their pastor. Louise told us: "Anyone who disagreed was labeled as having 'a critical spirit.' This psychological device crushed any disagreement, especially in congregational meetings. Even asking a question was denounced. This effective weapon kept people from questioning authority because they did not want to be labeled as having 'critical spirits.'"[29]

When we asked Louise the reason for this situation in a Bible-teaching church, she said, "It seemed to come from an extensive use of the 'chain-of-command' theory so popular then. You were under the authority of those above you, and you were to be obedient to that authority."[30]

Amazingly enough, authoritarian groups teach their members to obey their leaders—even if they are wrong. In case of error, God will hold the leaders accountable, not the disciples. As one teacher explains: "We as Christians do not obey those in authority because they are right; we obey them because they are in authority, and all authority ultimately stems from God Himself."[31]

But is this what God advocates?

## What God Says About Control

*1. Control violates one of Christ's specific commands.* When the disciples argued over who would be the greatest in the kingdom of God, they were jockeying for control. A pyramid structure would have suited them just fine, especially if all twelve of them could have been on top.

Jesus, however, had not come to set up such a structure. When he heard them arguing, he gently reminded them of his principles: "You know that the rulers of the Gentiles lord it over them, and their high officials exercise authority over them. Not so with you. Instead, whoever wants to become great among you must be your servant, and whoever wants to be first must be your slave—just as the Son of Man did not come to be served, but to serve, and to give his life as a ransom for many" (Matt. 20:25–28).

In speaking to church leaders, the apostle Peter advised: "Be shepherds of God's flock that is under your care, serving as overseers, . . . not lording it over those entrusted to you, but being examples to the flock (1 Pet. 5:2–3).

We should follow a leader who lives a godly, self-denying life with the welfare of his group in mind, not one who controls through an autocratic chain-of-command.

Author Bill Counts says: "Church elders [in the early church] were to shepherd, protect and care for their flocks. But there is no evidence they viewed themselves as having the kind of authority which [a certain group] invests in its leadership . . . . [The apostle] Paul instructs believers about every area of life—marriage, child-raising, jobs, sex, etc.,—

but he does not channel his instructions through elders . . . . The average believer was to make his own decisions before God in these areas."[32]

2. *Control fosters dependence on man.* When we rely upon a leader for guidance in our lives, we become dependent upon him rather than God. We then can come under his control. The apostle Paul saw this danger and warned, "You were bought at a price; do not become slaves of men" (l Cor. 7:23).

Moreover, the Lord warned us about trusting people: "Cursed is the one who trusts in man, who depends on flesh for his strength and whose heart turns away from the LORD. . . . But blessed is the man who trusts in the LORD, whose confidence is in him (Jer. 17:5, 7).

After fifteen years in the shepherding movement, Ron and Vicki Burks write: "The linchpin of the shepherding move- ment . . . is the concept of a 'committed relationship' to a 'personal pastor' or 'discipler'. . . . This doctrine has caused great pain and confusion for many followers and also for many of its proponents. The reason for the pain is simple—the doctrine is false! It is another gospel, usurping the rightful place of Jesus Christ in the life of the follower and obscuring the regenerating, sanctifying work of the Cross in his or her life."[33]

3. *Control denies the priesthood of the believer.* As Paul explained, "There is one God and one mediator between God and men, the man Christ Jesus" (1 Tim. 2:5). The writer to the Hebrews also affirmed that we can go directly to God with our problems, "Let us then approach the throne of grace with confidence, so that we may receive mercy and find grace to help us in our time of need" (Heb. 4:16).

We can go personally to God in prayer, recognizing that we are part of the priesthood of all believers.

The Reformation under Martin Luther had three great principles: The Bible as the final authority of faith and practice, justification by faith alone, and the priesthood of the believer. Bible scholars explain what is meant by such a "priesthood": "This doctrine meant that there was . . . one status before God common to all men and women, clergy and laity. Protestants opposed the idea that authority rested in an exclusive priesthood. . . . This did away with the need for the Virgin as mediator, the clergy as priests, and the departed saints as intercessors."[34]

God wants a direct, personal relationship with us. He says: "You also, like living stones, are being built into a spiritual house to be a holy priesthood, offering spiritual sacrifices acceptable to God through Jesus Christ. . . .

"But you are a chosen people, a royal priesthood, a holy nation, a people belonging to God, that you may declare the praises of him who called you out of darkness into his wonderful light (1 Pet. 2:5, 9).

*4. Control demands unquestioning obedience.* Most authoritarian groups use this verse as a scriptural basis for their position: "Obey your leaders and submit to their authority. They keep watch over you as men who must give an account" (Heb. 13:17).

However, the word *obey* in this verse does not mean forced submission to authority, according to expositor W. E. Vine. Rather, it is a voluntary obedience because a person has been persuaded or won over by a leader's godly life. The first part of the verse could be better translated, "Give assent to those who lead and guide you." The Greek meaning of the word has a softer quality than the English, according to Vine.[35]

The image is of a loving shepherd going before the sheep to seek out good pastures and clear waters. He lives a life of self-sacrifice, with the welfare of his sheep always in mind.

God never told us to obey our leaders unquestioningly. During the persecution of the early church, religious leaders commanded the apostles not to preach about Jesus. But the apostles responded, "We must obey God rather than men!" (Acts 5:29).

Furthermore, we are responsible to God for our actions, not to men. Biblical righteousness consists of obeying the commands of Scripture, of making right choices, of being accountable to God through faith in his Son. Therefore, we should never obey a leader who tells us to do something that goes against our consciences and the teaching of the Bible.

In fact, all of us will someday stand before the throne of God and account for our own words and actions. Our earthly leader will not stand alongside us and say, "Lord, you must not judge them for that. I told them to do it, so it was my mistake."

No, we will stand alone before God. Paul said, "For we must all appear before the judgment seat of Christ, that each one may receive what is due him for the things done while in the body, whether good or bad" (2 Cor. 5:10).

Finally, we should never give unquestioning obedience to any person. Such obedience belongs only to God. We are accountable to him, not to men.

*5. A shepherd cannot be a person's spiritual "covering."* He cannot protect another from error and satanic devices. The Bible teaches that God alone is our covering, our protection: "For you [God] have been my refuge, a strong tower against the foe. I long to dwell in your tent forever and take refuge in the shelter of your wings" (Ps. 61:3–4).

"He who dwells in the shelter of the Most High will rest in the shadow of the Almighty. . . . He will cover you with his feathers, and under his wings you will find refuge (Ps. 91:1,4).

In summary, we can assume that authoritarian control is a sign of false teaching. Author and teacher L. E. Maxwell wrote, "There is scarcely any lust . . . that can equal the passion of man for position, for ascendancy, for power . . . . So it has been ever since the fall of man: 'Every self, once awakened, is naturally a despot.'"[36]

President Abraham Lincoln agreed. In a speech during the Civil War, he said: "Our reliance is in the love of liberty which God has planted in us. Our defense is in the spirit which prized liberty as the heritage of all men, in all lands everywhere. Destroy this spirit, and you have planted the seeds of despotism at your own doors."[37]

## Questions
1. State the main reason for authoritarian structures.
2. Give six areas an authoritarian group seeks to control in the lives of its members.
3. What are three supposed benefits of control?
4. What do aberrant groups claim as the basis for their authoritarian ways?
5. Explain the reasoning behind unquestioning obedience.
6. What command of Christ's does control violate?
7. What do we mean by the "priesthood of the believer"?
8. Explain the word *obey* in Hebrews 13:17.

# Chapter 9
# Exclusivity

He drew a circle that shut me out—
  Heretic, rebel, a thing to flout.
But Love and I had the wit to win:
We drew a circle that took him in.
                                        —Edwin Markham

Novelist Daniel Defoe portrayed Robinson Crusoe as an English sailor who loved the sea. On one voyage, a hurricane broke masts, ripped sails to shreds, and wrecked the ship on a rocky reef. He and the rest of the crew climbed into a lifeboat, but it too was dashed to pieces on jagged rocks. All were drowned except Crusoe. Angry waves washed him ashore on a deserted, tropical island.

Cut off from the outside world, Crusoe lived for twenty-eight years with his dog, two cats, several goats, and a parrot. He rescued a native from cannibals who had come to the island to sacrifice victims. "Friday" became his faithful friend and servant. Crusoe built a tent from sailcloth, surrounded it with a stake fence, and added a cave to his shelter.

The isolated survivor was "prince and lord" of the whole island. "I had the lives of all my subjects [his animals] at absolute command," he wrote in his diary.

In like manner, an aberrant Christian group settles on an island of isolation in the ocean of traditional Christianity.

For instance, in the mid-1970s our shepherding movement church in Seattle emphasized home Bible-study groups, a

123

worthy goal. The difference between these small groups and those in mainstream evangelical churches lay in the fact that we all *had* to participate if we wanted to maintain our congregational-member status.

In our home group, we sang, prayed, and studied the Bible. We showed our caring for one another in tangible ways— giving food to a family when the husband was out of work. Contributing money for the wife's needed eyeglasses. Helping a young couple move into a new home and serving a potluck dinner afterwards. We all felt like one big happy family.

Sounds ideal? It was, at first. Gradually, however, the emphasis changed. Our pastors encouraged us to confine our social lives to our home groups—to have picnics, potlucks, outings, even vacations together. Soon we had little or no time for family or friends outside our closed circle.

This exclusiveness was not just confined to home groups. A few years before, our church had enthusiastically participated in annual citywide meetings for all denominations. Love and unity flowed freely as we gathered to hear special speakers. Now those meetings were no more. For the most part, we were an island, isolated from the mainstream of Christianity.

A far more extreme example of an exclusive, aberrant Christian group is the Branch Davidians. Members were "totally dependent" on leader David Koresh, according to cult-expert Rick Ross. Like Jim Jones, he "systematically brainwashed his followers and cut them off psychologically from the outside world." Therefore, in their confrontation with law-enforcement agents in Waco, Texas, they resisted "psychological pressure" and closed "ranks around" their leader.[1]

One reason for this was their "remnant" concept, rooted in Seventh-Day Adventism from which they came. According to Ken Samples of the Christian Research Institute, this "remnant" concept is the "central aspect of the Seventh-Day Adventist Church." They believe, he says, that "they are a special people with a special message at a special time." In fact, Sample says, "just like Luther, Calvin, and other reformers were a special movement in the sixteenth century, so they are a last-days' movement, a uniquely called-out people."[2]

The Branch Davidians go even further, says former member David Bunds. They believe they are "the remnant of a remnant." They are "even more select, more special, and more called of God for a special work."[3]

Here we see the sixth sign of an aberrant Christian group: exclusivity and isolation. It cuts itself off from those who disagree with its doctrinal stance. It has little or no fellowship with others in the Christian community.

## Why Groups are Exclusive

What are the reasons behind this phenomena? According to Christian counselor Linda Medill Hall, who has helped many from such groups, "a cultish leader has an independent spirit. He won't listen to anyone who challenges his teaching. He separates himself from close peer relationships so he is always the 'top dog' in control. He won't allow anyone to challenge him. He only aligns himself with those who agree with him or who live far away where his everyday life and church practices remain unobserved. He is not open to feedback or kindly suggestions.

"It's ironic," Hall continues, "that the very thing such a leader hopes to cure in his followers—independence—is the very flaw that makes him and his group untouchable and isolated from the rest of the body of Christ."[4]

Walter Martin, in his classic *The Kingdom of the Cults*, points out four psychological attitudes of cultists which foster isolationism. The same can be said of aberrant Christian groups:

1. *Close-mindedness.* Adherents are thoroughly convinced of the validity of their leader's teachings. They are "completely committed to the authority pattern" of their organization. Their minds are made up; they are not interested in exploring other views.

2. *Personal antagonism.* Followers of an aberrant leader want nothing to do with those who disagree with them. Their "genuine antagonism" is "on a personal level" with other Christians. Therefore, they reject individual believers as well as their beliefs.

3. *Intolerance.* Members of aberrant groups evidence "a type of institutional dogmatism and a pronounced intolerance for any position but their own," writes Martin.

4. *Spiritual blindness.* Because of the "factor of isolation," followers of an aberrant leader are blinded to blatant errors and inconsistencies in their teaching.[5]

Cult-watcher and author Dr. Ronald Enroth calls such

groups "churches on the fringe," even though they insist they are in the mainstream of Christianity. In reality, he says, they are estranged from "establishment evangelicalism" and "stand just outside the circle."[6]

This sort of isolationism has been creeping into churches for years, especially when a leader moves towards false teaching.

## What Exclusivity Does
### Exclusivity Breaks Christian Ties

A former member of the commune we have referred to in western Washington in the 1970s recalled that their leader, convinced them they were "a select little bunch." No one else could get into the group. "The door was sealed," she said. "We were exclusive. We were in God's favor above everyone else. We were going to save the world."

The leader planned to take his followers to Arkansas to buy land and to get into state government. The boys and young men would train as lawyers so they could control political offices. The rest would operate a communal farm to produce vast quantities of food.

"[The leader] said he was going to control the markets of the world," the former member explained. "People would starve in the terrible days ahead and would come to us for food. Anyone who didn't have money to pay for it would be shot."

This leader claimed he "was going to control the world with a handful of people," according to the former member. "He would say, 'When we all come to our place, when we all work together, we will have unbounded power. We can do anything.'"[7]

Other groups are also becoming exclusive. An author, in a *Spiritual Counterfeits* newsletter, says about one such church: "As . . . leaders delve deeper into little-known teachings of ancient church fathers, they tend to become more isolated from the twentieth-century body of Christ and stamp their movement with more of an elitist mentality."[8]

Josh, a student at the Bible school connected with a chapel in Washington, temporarily pastored a branch church in Oregon. As he became friends with other ministers, he took stock of teaching he had received at the school.

"I began to see some basic philosophies at [the church] that in my mind were harmful," Josh said. "There was a kind of elitist, exclusive attitude . . . . The idea was that we had more truth than any other people."

When Josh returned to Burien from Oregon in 1981, he wrote to the leaders of the chapel "detailing his opposition to the directions he felt the church was taking."[9] He and other dissidents charged that the church fostered elitism by saying that it was "the only sanctuary for a believing Christian." They also charged that it broke up marriages "when one spouse would accept the chapel's teachings but the other would not."

Josh and his friends also criticized "disfellowshiping— shunning persons deemed to be no longer walking with the Lord—for causing close friends and relatives to stop speaking to each other."[10] Each time this happened, the church bulletin inserted this notice along with the names of those involved:

> The Bible teaches us that those put out of the church are not to be associated with. We request all who attend [this church], not to associate with or discuss the matter with them. We do not expect family members to break natural ties with those whom we are forced to disfellowship, but those relatives who go to [this church] should be very careful not to treat them like brethren in the Lord or have spiritual fellowship with them.[11]

By March 1988, seven years later, the senior pastor's brother agreed with the dissidents. "It . . . became a prideful thing, . . an exclusive, elitist type of church," he said.[12]

Cult-watcher Ronald Enroth says that the pastor shared "his pulpit with few people outside a small circle of trusted associates." He urged his people to listen to his own taped sermons and warned against the use of other Christian tapes and books.[13]

The pastor of a growing suburban church near Seattle, Washington, held meetings every weeknight for the young men in the 1970s. A former member said, "He talked about our being 'the church' that was being perfected, and everybody else was outside. We were not to have contact with anyone, even our own families, because they weren't part of that group. He pulled away from everything and closed it in saying, 'We are it! Nobody else is included.'"

Jack, a young man who had formerly been part of the "in"

group, explained how their elitist mentality began: "[The pastor said that] the 'apostate' denominations were far from the truth, and this [teaching] was the truth . . . . Some of his railings against the 'apostate denominational dogs' were so intense, it was scary. They weren't spiritual like we were . . . . He preached that the denominational system frustrates the purposes of God. It dismantles; it's schismatic."

Donna, Jack's wife, told us how excited she was when she was first converted to Christ while a teenager. As she and her friends witnessed, "People were getting saved all over the [high school]."

But when she became deeply involved at the church, she no longer talked to others about her faith because "the doors were closing." The church's outreach stopped. When a young man joined the group, they commented, "He's the last one."

Why? "We were all in," Donna explained.

Jack told us about the leader's "vanishing doctrine." From Matthew 2 and 3, he taught that "Jesus [a type of the body of Christ] was taken down into Egypt [a type of the world] by Joseph and Mary to protect the testimony of Christ until he should be revealed at the proper time.

"So we didn't tell [people] we were Christians. We always spoke in parables. If they could figure it out, fine, but otherwise we were going to keep our identity as *the* body of Christ hidden."

In 1978, this "vanishing doctrine" was further put into practice when their leader decided they should all get away from the pressures parents and newspaper reporters exerted on them. Hence, they would go to St. Petersburg, Florida, to regroup and then on to establish a commune in Venezuela where they could be alone. The leader didn't want the young people to tell their families what they were going to do, so he came up with this idea: They didn't *go* to church. They *were* the church.

Donna explained how this was used to deceive others. "It was easy for me to tell my parents, 'We don't go to church anymore. Jack got this construction job in St. Petersburg, and we're going to move there.'

"My mom was thinking, 'Great!' She was glad I got out of the church and that Jack was not part of the eldership."

But that was not true. Jack and Donna were more involved than ever.

"Didn't you feel that anyone else was a Christian?" we asked them.

"We felt there were two types of believers—the overcomers and the carnal believers," Donna said. "[Carnal believers] were not going on with God . . . . They still had their salvation, but they weren't part of the bride of Christ. They would make it to heaven, but it [would] be by fire," Jack explained.

"Didn't you have fellowship with other Christians?"

"No, we didn't even know anybody else," Donna said.

"The only deliverance from . . . the influence of other people," Jack explained, "was to really get involved in what the 'fathering apostle' [leader] laid down for us."

"Everyone else was 'out to lunch,' Donna said, "and we had it all together."

"We were the 'firstfruits' of God's . . . church on the face of the earth. We were the only ones—ever," Jack added.[14]

## Exclusivity Breaks Family Ties

The natural result of such elitism and isolation is broken family ties. In one group, leaders encourage the breaking of ties between married partners when one is outside the group.

A former member, a medical doctor, wrote: "My wife was very unsympathetic to the whole thing . . . . I was told that if she would not come along, I might have to leave her."

Another man decided to leave the group after being in it for six years. His wife chose to stay. A church elder told her, "You're no longer under your husband's authority. A divorce will not be your fault, and your husband is going to hell. So why should you and the children follow him?'"[15]

The teachings of Jack and Donna's church also resulted in broken family ties. When they planned to marry, their leader said, "I look forward to just 'us' being at the wedding."

"We took that to mean we were to have only 'the body' [their group] there. [He] didn't say we couldn't have relatives," Donna said, but the implication was, "'If you really want to do God's will, this is what you'll do.' And we wanted to do God's will.

"I even [saw] my mom at the store one day when I was shopping for something for our wedding," Donna went on.

"She looked at me and said, 'You're like a stranger to me.'

"I didn't have anything to say to her. I didn't even tell her that I was getting married."

A girl from church told Jack's little sister at school that they were getting married, and she told her family. They invited the engaged couple for dinner. Afterward, Jack had to tell them that they weren't invited to the wedding.

"I was sick," Donna said. "I cried all the way home. But [we did it] for the sake of truth, for doing God's will, no matter how much it hurt."

"Did the leader tell you not to visit your families?"

"Oh, yes. He said to cut all ties," Donna replied.

"Why?"

"To go on with God. They weren't a part and were holding us down. They were 'strange flesh,'" Donna said.

## What God Says About Exclusiveness

God seems to have a different view regarding the isolation of believers. As we search the Scriptures, we see several principles emerge:

1. *Jesus prayed for unity among his people.* He said, "Holy Father, protect them by the power of your name—the name you gave me—so that they may be one as we are one" (John 17:11). He is praying for all believers—the church universal.

2. *Such unity is based upon the new birth and our union with Christ.* "Therefore," Paul told the Corinthian believers, "if anyone is in Christ, he is a new creation; the old has gone, the new has come!" (2 Cor. 5:17).

By virtue of our new birth, we are united with Christ. "Do you not realize," Paul asked, "that Christ Jesus is in you?" (2 Cor. 13:5).

3. *Unity is oneness of mind.* That was one characteristic of the early church, for "all the believers were one in heart and mind" (Acts 4:32).

Paul urged the Philippian believers to make his "joy complete by being like-minded, having the same love, being one in spirit and purpose" (Phil. 2:2).

The apostle Peter urged his readers to "live in harmony with one another; be sympathetic, love as brothers, be compassionate and humble" (1 Pet. 3:8).

4. *Unity is oneness of spirit.* "How good and pleasant it is," the psalmist said, "when brothers live together in unity!" (Ps. 133:1).

Although he did not know them personally at that time, Paul prayed that the Roman believers might have "a spirit of unity" so that "with one heart and mouth" they would glorify God (Rom 15:5–6).

5. *Unity is oneness of faith.* Paul explained that we have "one Lord, one faith, one baptism; one God and Father of all, who is over all and through all and in all" (Eph. 4:4–6).

6. *Unity is oneness of fellowship.* In the early days of the church, believers "devoted themselves to the apostles' teaching and to the fellowship, to the breaking of bread and to prayer." They had "everything in common." Every day they met "together in the temple courts. . . . praising God" (Acts 2:42, 44, 46–47).

Borderline groups not only become exclusive, but they often form communes to further separate them from "corrupting" influences.

Jesus, however, did not tell us to exclude ourselves from others. Instead he prayed, "My prayer is not that you take them out of the world but that you protect them from the evil one. . . . As you sent me into the world, I have sent them into the world" (John 17:15,18).

7. *Unity means no divisions.* Paul urged the Corinthian believers to "agree with one another so that there may be no divisions among" them and that might be "perfectly united in mind and thought" (1 Cor. 1:10).

Aberrant Christian leaders are usually independent. The examples we have considered all broke away from the mainstream of Christianity to establish their own groups. Thus, they do not have balanced peers to whom they are answerable for their actions.

The Book of Acts, on the other hand, shows the church at Antioch sending out Paul and Barnabas as a missionary team, an extension of the home base (Acts 13:1–3). Later, the two evangelists consulted with the entire council of apostles at Jerusalem regarding matters of doctrine (15:1–29).

8. *Marriages should be kept intact.* A leader should not break up a married couple. As Jesus explained, "A man will leave his father and mother to be united to his wife, and the two will become one flesh. So they are no longer two, but one. Therefore what God has joined together, let man not separate" (Matt. 19:5–6).

Paul urged that "a wife must not separate from her

husband. . . . And a husband must not divorce his wife (1 Cor. 7:10–11). In fact, he explained, "a woman is bound to her husband as long as he lives" (1 Cor. 7:39).

*9. Children should not break with their parents.* Paul says, "Children, obey your parents in the Lord, for this is right. 'Honor your father and mother'—which is the first commandment with a promise—'that it may go well with you and that you may enjoy long life on the earth'" (Eph. 6:1–3).

We Christians should ask ourselves the following questions:

1. Does our leader open himself up to peer relationships? Does he invite input from friends, fellow pastors, and a board? When he is challenged, does he thoughtfully consider suggestions?

2. Does he have an elitist mentality and act spiritually superior to others? Does he call our group "a special move of God" or "God's end-time ministry"? Does he feel he has a "greater anointing" than other leaders or an "inside track" to the Lord?

3. Does he isolate us from outside information? Does he urge us to listen only to his tapes and read his books and magazines or those which adhere to his doctrines?

4. Does he isolate us from other evangelical churches or parachurch organizations? Are we on the riverbank, watching mainstream Christianity go by?

5. Does he keep us so busy with services and group activities that we have no time or energy for family and outside friends? Does he tell us to break ties with family members who disagree with his teaching?

Let's not live within a closed circle, but draw a large one to include all true believers everywhere.

## Questions

1. What reasons are behind exclusivity in an aberrant Christian group?
2. What four attitudes foster isolationism?
3. Why are such groups sometimes labeled "churches on the fringe"?
4. How does exclusivity break Christian ties?
5. How does it break family ties?
6. What does God say about exclusivity?

# Chapter 10

# Demanding Loyalty and Honor

Power, like a desolating pestilence,
Pollutes whate'er it touches; and obedience,
Bane of all genius, virtue, freedom, truth,
Makes slaves of men, and of the human frame,
A mechanized automation.
                                    —Percy Bysshe Shelley

From the lush hills of England and white beaches of Australia and Hawaii, they came to the barren plains of Texas. Young and old. Black and white. A few were well-educated—a Harvard-trained lawyer, an engineer, a theology student, a minister, a social worker, a computer programmer. The rest were blue-collar workers, rock 'n' roll musicians, young couples with children, singles starting out in life. They had left their homes and possessions, their families and friends, their cultures and countries.

Despite the disparity of color and social status, they all were drawn to one man, David Koresh—a high school dropout with long hair, an unshaven face, wire-rimmed glasses, and rumpled jeans. They gave him their money, their wives and daughters, their loyalty and honor until death.

What was there about Koresh that drew such loyalty from his followers? His youth, his rock 'n' roll band, his guitar playing were all factors for some. His ability to reel off Bible verses and to preach in an exciting style played a part. His bold, confident manner made people believe whatever he told them, even that he was a second Jesus. But perhaps more importantly was his charm, his charisma, his magnetic personality that drew followers like fruit flies to ripe peaches.

Diana Henry, a twenty-six-year-old psychology student in England, heard the young prophet teach. She so fell under his spell that she convinced her mother, a nurse, and four siblings to follow him to Waco.

Diana's father, Samuel Henry, refused to go. "I told my family, 'You are on the road to destruction,' but they would not believe me," he said.

And he was right. Diana, her mother Zilla, two sisters, and two brothers died in the fire on April 19, 1993.[1]

Livingstone Fagan, a thirty-four-year-old former Seventh-Day Adventist pastor, walked out of the compound on March 19 and is under arrest. His children were released. His wife Evette stayed and died in the fire. Speaking from the McLennan County Jail, Fagan expressed sorrow that he hadn't died with his wife and friends. The fact that most members chose to burn together rather than surrender, he says, was "an indication of the strength of their faith."[2]

Or was it an indication of misplaced loyalty? Jeff and Kim, a young couple in our former shepherding church, told us that they talked to their home leader about questionable teaching and practices.

"If things keep on, this may become another Jonestown," Jeff said.

The home leader looked at them steadily. "Paradise or Jonestown—I'm committed all the way!"

When Jeff and Kim looked shocked, he added, "At least, Jim Jones' followers were totally loyal. Look at the average Christian—he sits unconcerned in his pew."

Such misplaced commitment brings us to the seventh warning sign of an aberrant Christian group—its demand for loyalty and honor.

## Sworn Loyalty

In an independent commune in western Washington during the 1970s and 1980s, the leader also demanded loyalty from his followers.

A former member explained to us: "Many times he had

us drink from a cup and swear our loyalty to him. This was one of his big things. It was like a communion service . . . .

"When people got out of hand or were disobedient or unruly," she said, "he would have us go through that act. This is where we got hooked. We then felt we could never go back on our word, our promise."

The charismatic leader attracted a number of educated people—a missionary, an ex-priest, an ex-nun, a professional man with an advanced degree in physics. These became his righthand leaders to carry out his wishes. Irene, the former member, says, "He had these people so enamored with him, so trusting, they would do anything for him."

According to Irene, the leader constantly sifted the ones "out of the group that he did not want there. They were not obedient to him and were seeing some things he didn't want them to see." He accomplished such sifting by closing the meetings and saying, "We're not going to have any meetings for a while. I'll let you know when we'll begin again." Then he never called those he knew were not loyal to him.[3]

## Loyalty Through Supernatural Means

When this leader first came to the West Coast from the eastern states, he lived with Irene and her husband for several months.

One evening, Irene went to bed early to read after a strenuous day as a secretary. The leader came to her open door and asked if he could dictate a letter to her.

When he was finished, he started to leave, but Irene said, "Wait a minute. Something's happening."

In her words Irene says, "I looked into his eyes, and he looked into mine, and there was a complete flow between us. His body looked like pure gold. I could see only parts of him. The room turned into this beautiful golden rain. I can't explain it to you, it was so glorious. I was stunned. I didn't know what to do.

"Then he started to prophesy. It was the highest prophecy I've ever heard in my whole life. We were in this state of absolute glory—the highest realm I've ever been in.

"Just then, I heard a knock on the door, and my husband came in. He asked what we were doing, and I said, 'Oh, honey, we've just had an experience I can't even explain to you.'

"But the spell was broken."[4]

Previously, Irene had had doubts about the leader and was not as loyal to him as the rest. But after this experience, she thought: *How could I doubt him after I've seen him in all this glory? How can I be disloyal to one so anointed of God?* So she continued to go along with him and his teaching.

At the beginning of his ministry in the Puget Sound area, the leader was "absolutely glorious, just beautiful," Irene says. "All the gifts of the Spirit were in operation. We were all free to prophesy. He himself did a lot of prophesying. He laid hands on people for healing." Strong ties between people and leader were formed during this time.

### Loyalty Through Work
One means this leader used to maintain loyalty to him and the group was hard work. He got everyone involved in the farm commune. They cleaned houses and planted gardens together. He kept them so busy that soon they had no private lives of their own.

He pushed his followers to the breaking point with very little sleep. They worked ten or eleven hours, then sat through his meetings for another two or three hours. If one of them dozed off, the leader humiliated him before the group. He made him stand without moving as punishment for not having the courtesy to stay awake while he taught.

Children sat almost motionless on the front benches during meetings. The youngest slept on blankets on the floor. He had such control over them that one rarely left to go to the restroom.

### Loyalty Through Physical Abuse
Another way this leader maintained loyalty was through physical abuse, especially of the older boys.

Irene tells what happened one day at a women's meeting: "Dan was a rebel. He would not bow the knee to the leader. Dan did something to anger him, so he took the boy to the basement. He put on boxing gloves, and he was going to have it out with Dan. The older man had perfected his muscles and had taken boxing lessons. This poor adolescent kid was humiliated and beaten by him. He came up the stairs bloody, with a possible broken nose, learning his lesson of obedience.

"His mother said, 'Oh, thank you! Thank you for doing that to Dan. He needed it.'

"[The leader] said, 'Yeah, I'm doing what you and Bill should have done when he was two years old.'"[5]

## Loyalty Through Secret Files

The leader also kept a file on each member of the group. Irene explains: "Every time a violation was made, he would write something up, and it would go in the person's file. We all knew that. Everyone was trying hard to be number one, to please him, and to get in his good favor. So instead of standing up to him and saying what they believed, they were intimidated. He could cow them with a look, he was so powerful."[6]

He could use information in a person's file for blackmail or to keep him from leaving.

## Loyalty Through Money

Even when some members wanted to leave, the leader forced them to stay and remain loyal to him. The children and young people were so attached to him because of his magnetic personality that they wouldn't go.

The parents were helpless. If they left, their families would be separated. They had given all their assets to the leader when they joined the group, so they would be penniless if they departed.

"You can't leave!" he would say. "I've got your money."

As Irene put it, "One way or another, each person was absolutely hamstrung. He couldn't move. It was like he had ropes around him. He couldn't get out. He had so much invested—his money, his children, his soul, everything. [The leader] had it all and had control of it."[7]

## Lifetime Loyalty

Lifetime loyalty is demanded in other present-day abberrant groups. In a *Spiritual Counterfeits* newsletter, an author tells of the devotion expected toward leaders of an authoritarian church: "The president . . . called upon each member to commit himself to the order for the rest of his natural life. Each one gladly and joyfully did this, with the exception of one who is no longer with the order."[8]

One of the top leaders of this group illustrated the type of loyalty and obedience he and other leaders expected. He asked an elder to stand and then asked, "If I told you to jump off a bridge, would you do it?"

"I would," the elder answered.[9]

*Loyalty to Fallen Televangelists*

Another example of misplaced loyalty was the way staunch supporters have stood by certain televangelists. In spite of evidence of sexual misconduct and lavish living, many were ready to welcome them back in leadership. As *Newsweek* reported: "Despite all the wretched excesses, the True Believers stood firm. 'I forgive [them] and hope they'll come back,' said [one] . . . . 'We all make mistakes.'"[10]

Another supporter who gave up to $10,000 a year to televangelists, was "irritated by all the criticism . . . . These people have done a lot of good in their lives," he says.[11]

Indeed, fallen leaders often receive considerable fan mail. Five hundred ministers sent letters of support to one fallen televangelist. Other fans offered him jobs as pastor and appearances on television shows. As he said, "I've been invited to be a clergyman in, I think, half the world's religions."[12]

## What God Says About Loyalty

What does God think about loyalty to our leaders or to our groups? Scripture gives these principles:

*1. God does not demand blind loyalty to leaders or groups.* Men being fallible, "the help of man is worthless" (Ps. 108:12).

The psalmist admonishes: "Do not put your trust in princes, in mortal men, who cannot save" (Ps. 146:3).

Man is fallible; God is infallible. Indeed, a leader and his group can be wrong, for "there is a way that seems right to a man, but in the end it leads to death" (Prov. 14:12).

*2. God says we should put our trust in him alone,* to give him our undivided loyalty: "It is better to take refuge in the LORD than to trust in man" (Ps. 118:8).

"Blessed is the man who makes the LORD his trust, who does not look to the proud, to those who turn aside to false gods [falsehood]" (Ps. 40:4).

So instead of looking to people, we should "fix our eyes on Jesus, the author and perfecter of our faith" (Heb. 12:2).

Author Dave Breese says: "Nothing is more tragic than blind loyalty, the tragic hypnosis which leads a foolish devotee of a given faith to stay with a leader or a movement which no longer is deserving of his confidence. Loyalty is a commendable virtue, but blind loyalty is a vice that can become fatal. The unclaimed bodies from Jonestown, Guyana, will be eternal testimony to this fact."[13]

Blind loyalty to a person is "a classic hallmark of authoritarianism," says cult-watcher Ronald Enroth.[14] Most certainly, we should not follow wrong teaching out of loyalty to a leader. As Fr. Dan Stewart observes, "Loyalty cannot be made a covering under which heresy is ignored."[15]

An editorial in *Christianity Today* agrees: "God has always used 'charismatic' men and women with great gifts of leadership to carry on his work in this world. But ultimate commitment is safely made only to God. No man or woman can be ultimately trusted."[16]

Breese explains further: "[The Christian] knows that the word *loyalty* is only applicable in a final sense when applied to our relationship to Jesus Christ Himself. The devotion that Christians have for one another is in loving response to the indwelling Holy Spirit, not submission to an enslaving external organization.

"It is a truism," Breese continues, "that the less truth a movement represents, the more highly it must organize. Truth has its own magnetism producing loyalty."[17]

"Our call," adds Stewart, "is to a larger loyalty to our Lord and to the whole Body of Christ."[18]

*3. We should trust the Bible, not the teachings of others.* The apostle Paul admonishes young Timothy to study the Bible: "Do your best to present yourself to God as one approved, a workman who does not need to be ashamed and who correctly handles the word of truth" (2 Tim. 2:15).

Why? Because the "Scriptures . . . are able to make you wise for salvation through faith in Christ Jesus." In fact, Paul said, "All Scripture is God-breathed and is useful for teaching, rebuking, correcting and training in righteousness, so that the man of God may be thoroughly equipped for every good work" (2 Tim. 3:16–17).

As one observer says, "We subject [a leader's] guidance to the perfect and infallible guide God himself has given us in Scripture."[19]

This is what Martin Luther did as leader of the Reformation. His stirring words still echo down the halls of time: "I do not trust in popes and councils since they often make mistakes. Unless I am shown out of the Bible, I neither can nor will take back anything. My conscience is a captive to the Bible, and I cannot go against my conscience."[20]

## Questions

1. Explain "covenant commitment" as practiced in some groups.
2. What means does an aberrant group sometimes use to maintain the loyalty of its members?
3. What does God say about blind loyalty to a leader or group?
4. Why should we give God our undivided loyalty?
5. What reasons does God give for the importance of Bible study?

# Chapter 11

# "New" Extrabiblical Revelation

[Cults] assert that God has spoken
outside or apart from the Bible.
—Dave Breese[1]

In the wireless shack of the new White Star liner *Titanic*,
First Operator John George Phillips stared at the pile of messages on his desk. He'd been tapping them out all day. Most
were frivolous greetings from passengers to folks back home.
By 11 p.m., he was tired, his nerves frayed.

Just when Phillips was making progress with his pile, the
liner *Californian* broke in with a loud message about icebergs.
She almost blew his ears off.

"Shut up!" he snapped back. "I'm busy!" He cut her off
before she gave her location.

He never sent the message to the bridge.

This was just one of four warnings of icebergs other ships
had sent the *Titanic* that day, starting at 9 a.m.

Lookout Frederick Fleet peered into the darkness from
the crow's nest at 11:40 that night. Star images glittered on
the cold, plate-glass surface of the Atlantic.

Suddenly, Fleet saw a dark image rising above the water
in the distance, drawing rapidly closer. He banged his
warning bell, lifted his phone, and called the bridge.

"What do you see?" someone asked.

"Iceberg right ahead!"

"Thank you," the voice answered calmly.[2]

Half a minute later, the *Titanic* collided with a gigantic mass of ice, shearing rivets and bending hull plates, making countless openings for ocean water to gush in.[3]

At 2:20 a.m., after two hours and forty minutes, the "unsinkable" ship reared its stern high, then slipped quietly beneath the frigid waters.[4]

And all because the crew of the *Titanic* failed to heed warnings.

For generations, men of God have warned believers to be suspicious of teaching which departs from the general body of truth that has been accepted by Christendom for the last two thousand years.

Today their voices warn even more loudly about the icebergs of "new" extrabiblical revelation taught by supposed evangelicals: a born-again Jesus. Little-gods Christians. Spiritual connections. A health-and-wealth gospel. Seed faith. Prophetic utterances on a par with Scripture. Undue submission to authority. Signs and wonders. "Slaying in the Spirit." Holy laughter. Barking like dogs. Roaring like lions.

If we fail to heed these warnings, we will run full-force into the icebergs of heresy and suffer the consequences.

The claim of "new" extrabiblical revelation is the eighth warning sign that a leader and his group have become aberrant.

## What is "New" Revelation?

What do we mean by "new" revelation? It may be a leader's overemphasis of some scripture verses or an adaptation of someone else's teaching. It may be prophecy, visions, or his own opinions. In themselves these are not necessarily wrong.

The danger comes, however, when such revelation is not planted firmly on the Word of God. When a leader is so filled with pride that he no longer spends much time with the Lord in prayer and Bible study, he allows Satan to deceive him. He may sincerely believe that what he is teaching is true, but he may be sincerely wrong.

While subtly brainwashing his followers with his own teaching, the aberrant leader downplays the need for personal Bible study. He may not come right out and say that it is unimportant, but he makes slighting remarks about this practice.

When a leader undervalues Scripture, deliberately or not, he effectively prepares people to look to him for guidance instead of to the Lord. His followers accept his teaching without question and without comparing with the Bible. Thus begins subtle brainwashing.

Once an aberrant leader breaks his followers of the habit of daily Bible reading and prayer, he then substitutes his own "new" revelation.

Such a leader saturates his preaching with his "new" truth. He then encourages his people to listen to his tapes and read his books, often to the exclusion of other material. This "truth," not available to outsiders is "pure, biblical Christianity restored," he says.

After hearing this teaching over and over, his followers accept it as truth.

These "truths" are based, as author Jeremy C. Jackson says, on a supposed "continuing revelation of new truths by the Spirit"[5] or extrabiblical revelation.

As author Dave Breese points out in *Know the Marks of Cults,* a cultic or aberrant leader asserts that "the Bible is only a part of the verbal revelation of God" and that he continues to speak today.[6]

An example is leader "Moses" David Berg of the Children of God cult. He felt God imparted a new revelation to him as his appointed prophet. After leaving his wife for his secretary, Berg now is in seclusion in Europe. From there he writes letters to his followers, who consider them as inspired as Scripture.

Another obvious example is the late Victor Paul Wierwille of The Way International. He claimed God audibly told him he would give him the first accurate knowledge of the Bible since the first century if he would teach it to others. His teaching books and "Power for Abundant Living" courses form the backbone of The Way theology.

## Substitutes for Scripture

Actual cults, however, are not the only ones who substitute "new" revelation for Scripture. Some supposed evangelical groups do it too.

What substitutes are used for Scripture? In this chapter,

we will focus on the following: false doctrine, prophecy, pronouncements and interpretations, visions, voices, and signs and wonders.

## False Doctrine

The waters of the present-day faith movement issue almost directly from the metaphysical healing cults, as espoused by the late author and teacher E. W. Kenyon (1867-1948). He diluted his evangelical theology with metaphysical concepts, especially from New Thought and Christian Science.[7]

Critics call faith-movement teaching "heretical" with "major departures from Christian orthodoxy." Notable among these teachings, they say, are:

- A deification of mankind, asserting that we are gods
- A deistic view of God, who must obey man's commands
- A demonic view of Christ, who was "born-again" in hell to rid himself of the "satanic nature" he acquired as a man
- A gnostic view of revelation, which denies the physical senses
- A metaphysical view of salvation, placing the atonement for our sins in hell rather than on the cross[8]
- Restoration of apostles and prophets
- Revelation knowledge

Furthermore, critics decry faith-movement practices, calling them "cultic":

- Financial prosperity gained through giving to the ministries of faith-movement teachers, which they call "planting seeds"
- Positive confession, by which man tries to manipulate God through confession of his name and Word
- Rejection of medical help when ill, sometimes risking death
- Sensory denial, by which man denies sensory reality, especially symptoms of illness[9]

Other present-day groups have added the following to the above list:

- Authoritarianism and submission to leaders
- Denial of the Trinity; a belief in "oneness" theology
- Deliverance of Christians from demons
- Signs and miracles

## Prophecy

We here refer to prophecy as one of the gifts of the Spirit as understood by charismatics or Pentecostals (see 1 Cor. 12 and 14), not the study of end times in Scripture nor preaching, as other evangelicals use the word.

Such prophecy is becoming more popular. One prophet, whom some call "the most anointed prophet . . . in the world today," predicts that soon "hundreds of thousands—perhaps millions" of prophets and apostles will perform healings, signs, and wonders, including resurrections. These prophets and apostles will emerge from "major streams of prophetic ministry."

This prophet claims the Lord visits him regularly—sometimes in heaven, sometimes on earth. Unusual phenomena often take place while he is speaking or prophesying—power surges that blow out electrical circuits and telephone systems, set off alarm systems, and short-circuit video cameras.[10]

And just what is prophecy to the charismatic/Pentecostal? Authors Dennis and Rita Bennett in their book *The Holy Spirit and You* say that "the gift of prophecy is manifested when believers speak the mind of God, by the inspiration of the Holy Spirit, and not from their own thoughts. It is supernatural speech in a known language" and is "always brought to a group of believers."[11]

The gift of prophecy ministers to Christians in three ways, say the Bennetts: "edification, exhortation, and comfort; or building up, urging on, and consoling" (1 Cor. 14:3).[12]

They tell believers: "Expect to prophesy. Ask Jesus to edify His Body on earth through you."

How is this done? Bennetts explain: "You may just receive a few words, and as you start to speak, more may come. You may see a picture in your 'mind's eye,' and as you start to talk about that picture, the words will come."[13]

Here is an example of a prophecy as given in a small Bible-study group:

The Lord would say to you today, "My children, I am the Good Shepherd. I will go before you and lead the way, step by step. Follow me closely, and I will direct your ways. Follow me as sheep follow their shepherd.

There are others who will follow you as you follow me, for sheep follow each other in a line. Thus saith the Lord.[14]

Critics contend that such prophecy, along with other revelatory gifts of the Spirit, is not for today. Bible scholar Merrill F. Unger in his book *The Baptism and Gifts of the Holy Spirit* says: "These [prophecy, tongues, knowledge] are the special gifts of the Spirit manifest in the early church enabling first-century assemblies to meet and have a preaching-teaching service before the New Testament was written and circulated among the churches."[15]

Unger feels that the apostle Paul "does not have in mind the ability through study of the prophetic Word to propound biblical prophecy. He means specifically an endowment of the Holy Spirit enabling a first-century believer, through extrabiblical revelation of the future, to declare truth now enshrined in the prophecies of the New Testament."[16]

Paul, says Unger, "describes that early period of partial, piecemeal revelation in the words: 'For we know in part and we prophesy in part' (1 Cor. 13:9). He is *not* speaking of today, but of his day, before the New Testament became available for study and exposition."[17]

Other critics object to a speaker using the phrase "thus saith the Lord" in connection with his prophecy, as if his words were a direct message from God and on a par with Scripture.

Neil Babcox, author of *A Search for Charismatic Reality*, agrees. As the young pastor of a charismatic church, he gradually developed "an uneasy sense" that the prophecies he heard, including his own, were "hardly worthy of the name." He admits: "The idea that they were the words of the living God was beginning to seem painfully ludicrous . . . . In my case, there were four simple words that played a decisive role in changing my heart: thus saith the Lord."[18] He explains further:

Thus saith the Lord. It is a rich, pregnant phrase. When a [Bible] prophet said "thus saith the Lord," he meant that the very word of God was being proclaimed, and that as such it was invested with divine authority. These words also convey the ideas of infallibility and purity—for could God's word be anything less? And as this phrase became ever brighter and more powerful to me, the prophecies that I had spoken and heard others speak paled and diminished to the point of nothingness.[19]

In most charismatic churches, prophecy usually follows "singing in the Spirit" and precedes the sermon. An aberrant leader, however, may use prophecy as a substitute for solid Bible teaching, calling it a "fresh word from God."

For instance, a small, charismatic church near Seattle, Washington, relies heavily on its pastor's prophetic utterances for guidance and teaching. As the pastor speaks with eyes closed, supposedly under the inspiration of the Holy Spirit, someone records his messages on tape, then later types and distributes them to the membership.

A former member told us that the church people studied and heeded his "anointed" words more than the Bible. In our talks with her, we realized that she did not know the basic stories and teachings of Scripture.

Another problem critics warn about is predictive prophecy. Yet it continues to be given in some charismatic circles.

One time, I (Agnes) went to a women's Bible study in a home. The guest speaker was a middle-aged lady wearing a white dress with her gray hair in a bun. Since I had met her before, she knew that my husband and I had returned from mission work because of my ill health. She gave a brief Bible study, then went to every woman in the room, giving individualized prophecies.

Suddenly, she whirled around and pointed her finger at me. "Agnes, God tells me that you're going back to the Philippines. But this time, you'll have a different ministry."

I sat there stunned.

That night as I lay awake in bed, my mind whirled. After having come through several years of illness because of life in the tropics, I wasn't eager to return.

Furthermore, her prophecy disturbed me. Why didn't she include my husband? Was John going to die soon? Would I have to go back alone?

The next day I told John what the lady had said. "I feel confused and upset," I concluded. "I thought prophecy was supposed to be encouraging."

"Hang it on a hook," John said. "If what she said is of God, it will come to pass. Otherwise, don't worry about it."

His sage advice calmed my troubled mind.

Some "prophets" seem to specialize in predictive prophecy. A young woman in California, for instance, told us about a house-church she and her husband had attended. Jane first became interested in this group when a friend took her to a charismatic Bible study and introduced her to Mary, the attractive leader.

Mary gave Jane a "special word from the Lord" and told her things about her past that only Jane herself could know.

Later Jane and her new husband moved to the city where the Bible study was held and attended regularly. At first, Paul, the husband, was wary of Mary's prophesying. But when she told him things about his past, he too became a believer in her powers and thought she was a woman of God.

As time went on, Paul and Jane, along with almost everyone else in the group, depended on Mary for guidance. When they contemplated changing jobs, selling houses, or making other major decisions, they went to Mary. She got quiet and supposedly listened to God. Then she gave them a prophecy, a "word from the Lord" just for their situations.

Although her husband shared the leadership of the group with another elder, it was Mary to whom the people looked most often. These men had lackluster personalities and were poor teachers. Mary, on the other hand, was dynamic and enthusiastic.

At first, most of Mary's directive personal prophecies seemed to come true. Then something happened. When a young woman became pregnant, Mary prophesied that the baby would be healthy and all would go well. Instead, the mother had a miscarriage.

Jane and Paul, along with several others, began to doubt Mary's prophetic powers. If she erred so badly in one matter, how could they trust her words again? After more of these instances, they became disillusioned and left the group, in spite of warnings of judgment from the prophetess.

In retrospect, Jane and Paul can see things more objectively.

They realize that the leaders gave little Bible teaching in the services. Most of the meetings were devoted to praise, worship, prophecy, and exhortation. They don't remember ever being encouraged to read their Bibles or to pray on their own.

Now they understand that the group's spiritual foundation was built on the shifting sands of prophecy rather than on the solid teachings of the Bible.

In another part of California, Jim and Betty were in a committed dating relationship. After hearing a prominent charismatic speaker, they asked him for a personal "word from God" for them. He laid hands on their heads and prophesied they would soon be married and be used together in a mighty way for God. Some months later, however, Betty met another man, fell in love, and married him.

Jim was confused about the prophecy given to Betty and him. In the future, how could he know what was from God and what was not?

What abuses can result from directive prophecy spoken as "thus saith the Lord"? Babcox claims it often bears "bitter fruit": "I have seen people married on the basis of guidance received from personal prophecies, only to be divorced a week later because of a terrible scandal. Many lives have been harmed by such prophetic guidance," he concludes.[20]

How can we know the true from the false? God has given a clear test to use in judging it: "You may say to yourselves, 'How can we know when a message has not been spoken by the LORD?' If what a prophet proclaims in the name of the LORD does not take place or come true, that is a message the LORD has not spoken. That prophet has spoken presumptuously. Do not be afraid of him" (Deut. 18:21–22).

## Pronouncements and Interpretations

An aberrant group can receive "new" revelation not only through prophecy, but also through its leader's pronouncements and interpretations. Instead of considering Scripture as their only basis for faith and practice, members go by what their leader says.

One group, according to an observer, teaches that it "has an authority at least equivalent to Scripture, since the church's leaders are the final interpreters of Scripture and must be *as implicitly obeyed* [emphasis in original] as God Himself."[21]

Basing their teaching on an ongoing revelation from God that did not stop when the canon of Scripture was complete, one of their leaders writes:

> The Holy Spirit's ministry of speaking to His church was not limited to the time of the twelve apostles. . . . To determine God's direction, you need both the spoken and written word and both the Scriptures and the Holy Spirit speaking in the church.[22]

Another leader also points out: "Too long have we merely followed Christian principles or directives God spoke to his people in years gone by. As believers we should expect to hear from God."[23]

According to the observer, however, members cannot decide whether a pronouncement is from God or not. The leaders alone do that. He observed: "Once decided upon, God's word to the church becomes as binding as Scripture itself."[24]

### Visions and Voices

An aberrant leader and group receives "new" revelation not only through prophecy and pronouncements, but also through supposed visions and divine voices.

In 1980, one televangelist said he had a vision of a 900-foot-tall Jesus at his bedside who promised he "would speak" to the leader's prayer partners and "through them . . . would build" a medical center.[25]

Another televangelist in one of his books tells about numerous visions he has had. In February 1959, while a patient in a hospital in El Paso, Texas, he was alone in his room during the dinner hour. He heard footsteps coming down the hall. "Someone dressed in white" and wearing sandals "came through the door . . . . It was Jesus!"

"Jesus" sat down by his bed and talked to him for an hour and a half, teaching him what sounds, curiously enough, like the tenets of the faith movement. Then he got up and opened the door, leaving it ajar.

The leader heard his footsteps fading "away down the corridor."[26]

In a newsletter to his followers, another televangelist wrote, "God woke me up at 4:00 in the morning. What he told me in an audible voice will change your life on March 17!" Then he described a vision he had:

In the Spirit I saw three little feathers float down, one by one, and land on my heart. As each feather touched my heart, God called out a word.

For each feather there was a single word, and those three words . . . are the keys to you receiving your miracle on March 17th . . . and they are: DECIDE, DECREE, and DECLARE.[27]

He explained that these words meant: "DECIDE what you want"; "DECREE it into existence"; and "DECLARE it to be so."[28]

## Signs and Wonders

Before enormous audiences while on television, one flamboyant televangelist has regularly made people fall "under the Holy Spirit's power" by blowing on them or waving his jacket at them.[29]

On January 20, 1994, an uncommon phenomena—"holy laughter"—took place among the 120 members at Airport Vineyard in Toronto, Ontario, Canada. These people fell on the floor "laughing, rolling, and carrying on." When news of this "spiritual outpouring" became known, people came from around the world to observe. Now they have gone home to take this new "message." The church in Toronto has grown to over one thousand members.[30]

Even more bizarre is the phenomenon of people roaring like lions and barking like dogs while supposedly engaging in "Spirit-filled worship."

Critics say that such "spiritual expressions and methodology are more at home in the occult than in Christianity."[31]

## What God Says About "New" Extrabiblical Revelation

*1. The Bible should be the foundation of our spiritual lives, not the words of men.* Christ spoke of it as the basis for all his teaching. He said he came to fulfill Scripture: "Do not think that I have come to abolish the Law or the Prophets; I have not come to abolish them but to fulfill them" (Matt. 5:17).

*2. The Bible is eternal; man's teaching will pass away.* We need to make Scripture our foundation because of its eternal nature. Christ said, "Until heaven and earth disappear, not the smallest letter, not the least stroke of a pen, will by any means disappear from the Law until everything is accomplished" (Matt. 5:18). Again, "Heaven and earth will pass away, but my words will never pass away" (Matt. 24:35).

The psalmist agreed when he said, "Your word, O LORD, is eternal; it stands firm in the heavens" (Ps. 119:89).

*3. The Bible is divinely inspired.* Jesus said to his opponents, "Have you not read what God said to you?" (Matt. 22:31).

The apostle Peter had a similar attitude toward Scripture. He said, "Above all, you must understand that no prophecy of Scripture came about by the prophet's own interpretation. For prophecy never had its origin in the will of man, but men spoke from God as they were carried along by the Holy Spirit" (2 Pet. 1:20–21).

The apostle Paul likewise proclaimed Scripture as divinely inspired when he said, "All Scripture is God-breathed" (2 Tim. 3:16).

The psalmist David said that God's Word was true: "Your righteousness is everlasting and your law is true" (Ps. 119:142). "All your words are true; all your righteous laws are eternal" (Ps. 119:160).

Since God's Word is perfectly true, it acts as a level to reveal false teaching. If we have laid solid, straight foundations of the Bible in our lives, then when we add something that is out of line, we can see that it is crooked. The prophet Isaiah explains: "To the law and to the testimony! If they do not speak according to this word, they have no light of dawn" (Isa. 8:20).

*4. Heretical teaching is satanically inspired.* Paul proclaims: "The Spirit clearly says that in later times some will abandon the faith and follow deceiving spirits and things taught by demons. Such teachings come through hypocritical liars, whose consciences have been seared as with a hot iron" (1 Tim. 4:1–2).

*5. God tells us to sift truth from error.* We should not accept any teaching without searching the Scriptures to see if it is true.

In fact, Luke, the writer of the Book of Acts, commended the believers at Berea for comparing Paul's teaching with Scripture: "Now the Bereans were of more noble character than the Thessalonians, for they received the message with great eagerness and examined the Scriptures every day to see if what Paul said was true" (Acts 17:11).

Author Jeremy C. Jackson explains the need for such sifting when he writes:

> When we see that all heresies are partial or more total distortions of the truth, that they reflect spiritual willfulness, and that none of us is so spiritually strong as to be immune from error, then we have to be very grateful for a written revelation of God's truth to protect and guide us.[32]

*6. We should read and study the Bible for ourselves.* Church history shows us that when believers neglect personal Bible study and prayer, the result is spiritual malnutrition. They then become easy prey for false doctrines. Just as prisoners of war are kept docile through starvation, so Christians in aberrant groups go along with whatever leaders say, scriptural or not.

We need to remember that a state church discouraging personal Bible reading brought on the Dark Ages. Leaders told their people to listen to and obey the teaching of the church alone. Reading the Bible was heretical.

Yet Scripture clearly states that we are made spiritually strong by personal study, not by merely listening to or reading someone else's ideas about what the Bible says.

The apostle Paul told the Ephesian Christians: "Now I commit you to God and to the word of his grace, which can build you up and give you an inheritance among all those who are sanctified" (Acts 20:32).

The blessed man of Psalm 1 becomes strong by meditating on God's Word day and night—like a tree drawing sustenance from a life-giving stream.

However, Satan, knowing that the Bible is the main source of our spiritual strength, will do everything in his power to keep us from it. Paul warned young Timothy about false teachers and urged him to study the Bible for himself: "Evil men and impostors will go from bad to worse, deceiving and being deceived.

"But as for you, continue in what you have become convinced of, because you know those from whom you learned it, and how from infancy you have known the holy

Scriptures, which are able to make you wise for salvation through faith in Christ Jesus" (2 Tim. 3:13–15).

In fact, God says we are to meditate on his Word constantly. Here is his simple formula for spiritual success: "Do not let this Book of the Law depart from your mouth; meditate on it day and night, so that you may be careful to do everything written in it. Then you will be prosperous and successful" (Josh. 1:8).

So we should question a leader who says, "There is no need to close our eyes when we pray. It is better to close our minds. There is no need to explain or expound the word; simply pray the word. Forget about reading, researching, understanding, and learning the word." He even encourages his people to read it backwards.[33]

We should question a leader who says, "Christ never intended to start a religion based on a book . . . . I believe in a continuing revelation."[34]

Let's commit ourselves to a fresh study of the Scriptures. A quick look across the pages of church history will reveal the results of reading, believing, and obeying God's Word.

Consider the psalmist David. He spent hours in prayer and reading the Scriptures as a shepherd in quiet pastures. Out of those times came his psalms, which have blessed untold numbers.

Hudson Taylor spent hours studying the Bible and praying. In his heart was born the China Inland Mission (now the Overseas Missionary Fellowship), which has won thousands to Christ in the Far East.

C. T. Studd, a wealthy and famous athlete at Cambridge University in England, came to Christ as a young man. He began a lifelong habit of rising early to spend time with God in Bible study and prayer. Set aflame for the Lord, he founded the Worldwide Evangelization Crusade, which has made an impact around the world.

Amy Carmichael, missionary to India, became bedridden. She spent long hours reading her Bible and praying. Out of her communion with God came poems and books which have blessed the Christian world for years.

In fact, evangelist D. L. Moody said, "I never saw a useful Christian who was not a student of the Bible. If a person neglects the Bible, there is not much for the Holy Spirit to work with."

Author and minister Samuel Chadwick wrote in the last century:

> I have guided my life by the Bible for more than sixty years, and I tell you there is no book like it. It is a miracle of literature, a perennial spring of wisdom, a wonder of surprises, a revelation of mystery, an infallible guide of conduct, and an unspeakable source of comfort. Pay no attention to people who discredit it, for I tell you that they speak without knowledge. It is the Word of God itself. Study it according to its own directions. Live by its principles. Believe its message. Follow its precepts. No man is uneducated who knows the Bible, and no one is wise who is ignorant of its teachings.

Let's not let anyone rob us of this treasure—God's holy Word.

## Questions

1. What do we mean by the term "new" extrabiblical revelation?
2. What dangers are inherent in such "revelation"?
3. Name some substitutes used for Scripture?
4. Define "prophecy" as used in this chapter. How does it differ from the study of end times?
5. What is the value of prophecy from a charismatic or Pentecostal viewpoint? What problems do critics see in its use?
6. What dangers lie in a leader's personal pronouncements and interpretations of Scripture?
7. Discuss the visions and voices some leaders claim they have seen and heard.
8. What does God say about Scripture? What does he tell us to do?

# Part III:

# Mainstream or Wreckage?

# Chapter 12

# How to Get Out of the Whirlpool

While I see many hoof marks going in,
I see none coming out.
It is easier to get into the enemy's toils
than out again.
—Aesop, *The Lion, the Fox, and the Beasts*

Karen, an enthusiastic twenty-one-year-old, had lived in one of our shepherding church's community houses in the university district. Eager to grow spiritually, she entered wholeheartedly into life with other young people. She loved the rousing song fests and pep talks by their leaders. Everyone seemed loving and caring.

As time went on, however, Karen felt stifled under the pressure to conform. She chafed under the taunts of her roommates.

"Studying your Bible again, huh?" they said. "Don't you know it's more important to *live* the life than to fill your mind with head knowledge?" They scarcely looked at their Bibles, since they depended on their leaders for spiritual teaching.

After numerous bad experiences, Karen left the community house and the church.

I saw her at Linda's home one evening. She was broken and disillusioned. "I'll never trust anyone again!" she said with a sob. "I can't believe I was so deceived!" She had given the church and community her all. Now the pieces of her life lay shattered around her.

Linda and I sat with her on the carpet while she cried her heart out. It took months of praying for and counseling Karen before she regained her spiritual composure and had the courage to look for another church home.

Although we had almost no contact with anyone still in the church, we increasingly ran across others who had left. We didn't realize there were so many.

When we asked them for details, we heard some interesting stories. Almost all had questioned the validity of the heavy-handed control exercised by the leaders. Any who had the nerve to take this concern to the senior pastor suffered his anger and accusations. Most of them went through trauma and depression.

This is true not only for those who had left our church, but for those who come out of any aberrant group.

One example is from the turn of the century. Mrs. Fred Caillat from Tacoma, Washington, fled the commune in Maine called "Shiloh" with her three children in 1906. She had lived there six years with her husband, a formerly prosperous plumber.

He refused to leave with her and sailed to Jerusalem with leader Frank Sandford.

"I left because I could not endure the life there any longer," Mrs. Caillat said in a newspaper interview. "I was awfully frightened and fought through a severe battle with my fears. I was assailed with doubts whether I would not lose my soul and ruin my family if I left Shiloh. We are taught so strongly that breaking with Shiloh means breaking with God that I almost lost the little courage I had worked up."

"Do all at Shiloh believe that, Mrs. Caillat?" the reporter asked.

"Oh, yes. That is the beginning and end of everything there. One is not a Shilohite at all who does not accept that. I remember once in the chapel when Mr. Sandford was leading a meeting, he said, 'How nice it is here! We pray, and God hears our prayers. God is real to us. Think of those who have left the work, Mr._____, Mrs._____,' and he named several prominent ones who had left, especially emphasizing one man who has written against the work.

"That sort of thing is enough to frighten people, especially people so nervous and strained up as they are there.

"Then someone wrote me that Mr._____, who had left the work, was miserable and confessed that he was lost. I found out since that it was a lie, but it had a strong influence on me to make me fear.

"I couldn't stand it, though, and I decided to leave in spite of my fears. God gave me faith to believe that he would hear my prayers, even if I did leave. So when my mother wrote me that she would send me a ticket to come to California, I packed my things and waited for it to come.

"One night, Mr. Emmons, who had charge of the Higgins' House to which I had been sent for punishment for speaking my mind, learned of my intention and came to my room and talked to me very severely for a long time. I should think an hour. He tried to find out where I got my money I had been spending for myself and the children.

"My mother had recently sent me ten dollars. I would not tell him.

"He was very angry. He said I must have begged it, as God would never send money to such a rebel.

"I told him I had never asked anybody for a cent.

"Then he said, 'Don't you think you ought to have asked Mrs. Emmons' permission before you went shopping?'

"I told him, 'No.'

"Then he tried to frighten me, talking so fiercely that he fairly shook his fist in my face. 'The idea,' he said, 'spending money for food when the kingdom is in debt!' Then he said, 'Suppose your baby should die tonight?'

"I said, 'Let it die; it will only die by inches, anyway.'

"'Suppose your boy should die before morning?'

"'Let him die. He can't suffer any more than he suffers now, dying slowly.'

"'Suppose you meet with a railroad accident? God has lots of ways to run you down.'

"Well, this did not frighten me and did not make me feel like staying there any longer. So after breakfast next morning, I went to Mr. Cartland as he was passing and asked him if I could come to his home and stay till my ticket came.

"He is a very kind man, and he said I could.

"So I packed what things I had so I could send for them, put the baby and a few parcels in the baby carriage, and with the two other children started to walk to his house, about a mile away and uphill.

"I was very weak, but the thought of freedom lent me strength.

"Just before I reached the house, I heard a team on the gallop following me. It was two of the ministers, Mr. Jewell and Mr. Tupper, and they were whipping their horses to overtake me. They stopped me and held me there for two hours, trying to coax and then to frighten me into returning.

"I was very tired from the walk, and my old heart trouble came on with the excitement, and I thought I should drop in my tracks.

"They looked at me at first as if they thought I would be ashamed; then they threatened me; and at last left me in great anger, as if I was doomed.

"Well, I found my way to Mr. Cartland's and the whole family was very kind to me. I was there nearly three weeks till my ticket came; and soon after I left, Shiloh sent a team up there after my things.

"Looks as if they thought they could get me, but were too late. That is how I got away."[1]

A contemporary example shows the same courage needed to leave an aberrant group. Jack and Donna were among ninety young people from a suburban church near Seattle, Washington, who had moved with their leader to St. Petersburg, Florida, in April 1978. They planned to regroup there before going on to Venezuela to found a commune. But as they got involved in buying property and construction work, they put their plans on hold.

After a hot, muggy summer and fall, the leader decided to bring his large sailboat from its moorings in Puget Sound and ready it for taking the group and cargo to Venezuela. He and three of his men returned to the Seattle area in midwinter, outfitted the boat, and started off.

They had a perilous trip down the West Coast to California, where the leader resolved to put in new engines before continuing through the Panama Canal. He called the commune in Florida and asked Jack to fly out and help them. Jack went, expecting to be back shortly with the boat and crew.

When they reached southern California, the leader fell in love with sunny San Diego. He and his closest friend explored the city, while Jack and the other men worked on the boat.

Weeks went by, and still they were delayed. It seemed the leader wasn't too anxious to get home to Florida. Jack, however, was homesick for his wife, especially since they were newlyweds. Although the leader and his friend called their wives regularly, Jack and the other men were not allowed to do so.

In retrospect, Jack is thankful for that difficult time. It gradually made him realize that his leader was not as wonderful as he had thought. Jack had almost idolized him. Now he saw him for what he was—an egocentric with real problems.

At the end of the four-month separation, Jack and Donna stood at the window of their darkened room in the big, old house in St. Petersburg. A large, yellow moon silhouetted palm trees in the distance. They could hear water running in the bathroom below and a child crying upstairs. The dank smell of old cigarette smoke from previous tenants rose in their nostrils.

Jack pulled his wife towards him and searched her face in the moonlight. "Donna," he whispered, "we've got to get out of here! I can't take it anymore."

"I know. I can't either."

"I've been seeing the stratification between us and our 'noble' leader. He drives a Lincoln Continental and controls our gas station. Our food service. Three houses. Our housing complex. The eighteen-unit apartment building. And he lives in the nicest house, with central air-conditioning. And how do we live?"

"Let me tell the ways," Donna said. "In a big, dilapidated house built in the 1920s. Cockroaches everywhere. Walls so stained with smoke that when you take a picture off, you can see where it's been. Decrepit furniture. Urine on our mattress and carpet, and they wouldn't let us clean them. Remember what our leader said, 'Just turn the mattress over?' . . . But how can we leave? We don't have any money."

"I don't know, but we'll think of something."

"Oh, Jack," she whispered as she hugged him, "I'm so afraid. What will happen to our marriage, to our finances? Remember those warnings of judgment if we get out from under our leader's 'covering'?"

The stocky young man turned again to the window. *Yes, what would happen? Do we have the courage to follow through?*

Jack was so disturbed, he went through his days like a zombie. He worked at his construction job and ate meals without speaking.

One day in a shopping mall, he and Donna met a couple who had left two months before. Jack told them about their questionings.

"Everything you've been seeing is true," the other young man said. "The whole system is wrong."

"But we're under the 'covering' of the group now. What's out there from under it?"

Jack's friend scanned their anxious faces and replied with a twinkle in his eyes, "Fellowship with Jesus."

His simple words struck them like an electric shock. Scales of deception fell from their spiritual eyes, and they melted inside. They suddenly realized how far they'd strayed from the close fellowship with the Lord they once had. They had allowed their leader to stand between Christ and them.

On the way back from the mall, Jack and Donna decided to leave. They went to their room and packed behind the closed door.

Because of the commitment they had signed, they knew they couldn't get back the twenty thousand dollars they had given the group. They also had been signing their paychecks from work over to the organization. Now they put stop payments on a few, so they would have enough money to get back home.

Jack and Donna still had moments of indecision. To leave meant not only financial, but psychological tearing because of their close relationships with others in the group.

Later, Jack explained to us, "The memory of all the burned and mangled bridges that we had left behind at home seared our consciences and hurt our hearts. We realized what severe actions we had taken in our supposed pursuit of God—actually in following our leader."

"Once we entertained the thought of leaving," Donna added, "I knew we could never turn back. We could never trust or respect our leader again. Sometimes we asked each other, 'What about all these sincere people? We hate to leave them here. But we have to.'"

Finally an assistant leader called Jack in. "Something's wrong with you. What's up?"

"I've got problems."

When the assistant insisted that he explain, Jack admitted, "We're leaving. We'll be gone by one o'clock tonight."

He and Donna finished packing, then moved into the home of the friends they had met in the mall.

Their emotions seesawed between elation and regret. One day Jack almost decided to return, then thought better of it. He sat down and cried bitter tears. He felt confused, torn in pieces.

Daydreaming about future possibilities helped them make the final mental break. The group hadn't allowed anyone to attend universities, although a few took vocational classes. Now the young couple had the freedom to do some wishful thinking.

On a long walk together one afternoon, Jack said, "Wouldn't it be neat to go to school—to a real university?"

"It would!"

They stopped and stared at each other with sparkling eyes before resuming their stroll. Their own decisions! They relished the freedom.

"What classes would you like to take?" Donna asked.

"First, I'll have to decide what my major will be. What do you want to take?"

"I don't know. I haven't even let myself think along this line for so long," Donna said.

"Well, we can dream, can't we? At least, it gives us something to look forward to."

At last, Jack, heart pounding, called his father. The two hadn't talked for a long time.

"Dad," he said with a catch in his voice, "we're coming home."

## What to Do

If you feel that the eight warning signs fit the church or group you are in, you may wonder what to do about your situation. Here are some suggestions:

*1. Consider leaving.* Some stay in a situation with borderline teaching and activities simply because they don't like to pull out. Others don't know of a better place to go. Still others hope they can pray the problems through.

They're like drugged flies caught in a spider's web. They know something is wrong, but they're not sure what. Yet they feel comfortable in the confines of their bonds. To leave is frightening. Where will they go? What will they do? And what about all their friends and family with them in the web?

They may struggle in their bonds, but soon find the effort tiring. It is easier to stay and doze in the sun.

Meanwhile, the spider winds more silky strands around them—until it's too late.

Remember that the spider is Satan himself. The leader is merely a body he uses. If he can get a foothold in the leader's life, he can deceive him, then use him to deceive others. Through him, the devil deftly spins strands of control around the numbed followers until he has them in a tight web of bondage.

Eventually, a demonic bondage may take over. Those in the web—earnest Christians though they be—develop film over their spiritual eyes so they cannot see their perilous position.

The one word of advice we have for those caught in such a web is—leave! God warns that he will punish your proud leader, for "pride goes before destruction, a haughty spirit before a fall" (Prov. 16:18). So unless you want to be a part of the leader's destruction, you'd better get out quickly.

Punishment from God takes different forms. Frank Sandford spent years in prison. Jim Bakker did the same. Such leaders lose their positions, their families, their friends, their reputations, often their health.

On the other hand, members of a congregation or organization sometimes stand together against an erring leader and put him out instead. We know of one church that did this. In effect, they said to their pastor, "We don't like where you're taking us, and we refuse to go any further with you. You're going to destroy this church. So either you change your ways or leave."

The pastor left, and the church is recuperating.

*2. Recognize and renounce the false teaching and cultish bonds.* Any truth pushed too far can become heresy. If the teaching you received does not line up with God's Word, you need to recognize it as heresy and renounce it.

Most people who pull out of aberrant groups feel as though they've been ground through a food processor. They are broken to bits, stunned, confused, not sure what happened to them.

That's why it's important for you to recognize what was wrong and to call it for what it is. You may feel guilty doing this. You may not be sure who was wrong—the group or yourself. This is especially true when large numbers of people are still in the church.

But remember, consensus doesn't make it right. Hitler had a huge following, too.

That is why it is important to share your story with an objective, caring Christian friend or counselor, then immerse yourself in reading the Bible. As you expose what happened in darkness and hold it up to the light of God's Word, the spiritual haze can lift. Gradually, the group's unhealth and twisting Scripture to fit its pet doctrines will eventually become clear.

If the bondage you were under was extreme, you may need help in breaking it and the ties with your former leaders. Here is a sample prayer to say either by yourself or with someone:

> In the name of Jesus Christ of Nazareth, I renounce the heresy I've accepted. I put it out of my mind, soul, and spirit and will have nothing more to do with it. I break every tie my soul has had with _____ (pastor/leader) in the mighty name of Jesus and declare that I am free. Lord, now fill the void with your Holy Spirit.

*3. Forgive those who have hurt you.* Although you may find it difficult to forgive if you've been wounded deeply by those you loved and respected, it is the only way to total healing. Otherwise, bitterness will fester like an ulcer within you. The pain will be so great, it will be all you can think or talk about.

Go over each specific instance of hurt, and forgive those involved. You may want to make a list of the occasions and people. Remember that bitterness is just as wrong in God's eyes as what others did to you, and it gives Satan a foothold in your life.

"If you forgive men when they sin against you," Jesus said, "your heavenly Father will also forgive you. But if you do not forgive men their sins, your Father will not forgive your sins" (Matt. 6:14–15).

*4. Pray for your former group and its leaders.* Jesus also said to "bless those who curse you, pray for those who mistreat you" (Luke 6:28). Those you have left behind usually are fine people who love the Lord and think they're doing his will. As you pray for them, you will find forgiveness and love flowing towards them.

The Lord may lead you to join with others on a regular basis to intercede for these leaders and their people. If they truly are deceived, they need to have their eyes opened.

Above all, make sure that your footprints lead out of the den of deception, not back into it.

## Questions
1.  Write down the eight warning signs of an aberrant group given in this book.
2.  Why do some stay in aberrant groups, even when they see warning signs? Why should they leave?
3.  Why should they renounce false teaching and break soul ties with former leaders?
4.  What's the purpose of forgiveness?
5.  Why is prayer for one's former aberrant group and its leaders important?

# Chapter 13

# How to Get Back into the Mainstream

> Build today, then, strong and sure,
> With a firm and ample base;
> And ascending and secure
> Shall tomorrow find its place.
> —Henry Wadsworth Longfellow,
> "The Builders"

Today many "cruise ships" of aberrant leaders are stuck in the slough of deception. Earnest Christians are abandoning ship and are piling into lifeboats to head for safety.

But they thrash their oars around, wondering which way to go. They are disillusioned. Traumatized. Depressed. Grieving. Bitter.

How can they get back into the mainstream of Christianity?

This is not a new phenomenon. It has been repeated through the years. Consider the story of "Shiloh," a commune in Maine at the turn of the century.

The Reverend Nathan Harriman, who brought most of his church members from Tacoma, Washington, in 1900, left Shiloh after three years. In an article entitled, "The Inside Story of Sandfordism and Shiloh," for the *Lewiston Evening Journal,* he wrote regarding leader Frank W. Sandford:

People blindly bow at his shrine and believe that he holds their destinies, for time and eternity. And he does, until they are courageous enough to assert their manhood and dare to think for themselves; then the spell breaks quickly enough, though it is a long time before they get wholly free from the terror . . . . Can any one [sic] wonder that my blood boils at this imposition upon God's dear sheep, now that He has freed me? None who have tasted the slavery will wonder. All who have known the torture will thank God that I speak strongly.[1]

Sandford thought those followers who questioned him were "rebellious" and "snared" by the devil. They then had two choices—to relent and submit to him, "the prophet," or to leave Shiloh in disgrace.

"Many go out hopeless," Harriman said, "and plunge into sin as a result, to drown their sufferings."

Anyone who left the commune was considered demon-possessed or insane, according to Harriman. Sandford's teaching and influence held those who remained and damned those who went. He taught that if a person prospered after leaving, it was proof that Satan prospered him. If he did not prosper, God's judgments were falling upon him.[2]

Sandford told one man who was leaving that he had "no right to use the blood of Jesus, no further right to any of the benefits of the gospel."

In despair, the man later wrote Harriman, "I do not profess anything, do not pray, and scarcely ever read my Bible . . . . I have spells of crying whenever I get to thinking the situation over." With a heart still hungry for God, he urged Harriman to come to see him and others who had left. "I want to know the truth. I don't know what to believe. If I can get saved independent of Mr. Sandford, I want to know it. . . . I don't want to believe a lie."[3]

Another man who left Shiloh wrote Harriman:

I had an awful oppression come over me Monday, and I felt terribly discouraged and blue. The thought came to me that Shiloh was praying for me perhaps, and all hell was surging upon me. . . .

I see the importance of a place where Shiloh people

[who leave] can go to. The oppression that comes on a person is awful at times. It takes time to establish a person on the gospel after having had the terrors of the law for years. I wish you could get a home. I need the mutual help. A visit to you helps me wonderfully. I thank God for the courage you have given me, and thank you, too.[4]

When Fred G. McGregor of Lowell, Massachusetts, was taking his daughter away from Shiloh, Sandford told them that if they left, they'd "be damned and go to hell."[5] This was said in spite of McGregor's gift of the white-and-gold "gospel chariot" a few years before.

Escape is only the first challenge in rebuilding one's life. When Jack and Donna left the commune at St. Petersburg, Florida, they returned to the Seattle area.

"Our first year back," Jack recalled, "we weren't involved in church at all. We had difficulty sorting things out."

"It was a slow process," Donna added. "I wanted everything to be okay, all better, no more hurts. But it wasn't that way. I wondered, *What do I have to do? Throw out everything I've learned and start completely over?* I didn't want to do that. It would be too hard. Almost every week, some doctrinal point came up, and I'd have to face it and ask, *Do I believe this anymore? What is the truth?*"

"I really lost my trust in God because of what happened," Donna admitted. "I had faith in him in my early Christian life, but eventually that trust got transferred to a man [their leader] who disappointed me. I felt that God had disappointed me. I was so afraid that he would put me through something like that again if we ever got involved in another church. Even when Jack went looking, I didn't go. I said to him, 'You go and scout it out.'

"Later, I realized that when I decided not to go to church, I also decided to cut off God's influence in my life," Donna continued. "And that's sin."

"When we left," Jack added, "I really needed to know what was wrong with their teaching. We're still sorting out doctrinal things, but the healing didn't start until I got back in communication with God. It took two years to realize that he hadn't forsaken me.

"But God in his infinite mercy in spite of our error, moved

us to find another church. For a while, we just sat and listened and let the Lord heal us."

Then the young couple worked on healing severed relationships with family and friends. When Donna finally realized the hurt she had caused her parents, she went to them in repentance. "I'm so sorry," she said. "Can you forgive me?"

"I've already forgiven you," her mother answered.

They hugged while the tears flowed.[6]

## What to Do

After leaving an aberrant group, what can you do to rebuild your spiritual life and to keep you from following another "evangelical superstar"?

*1. Have a regular devotional life.* Read and study your Bible every day. God's Word is the foundation of your Christian life and will keep you from going astray again. It is also like a bath, for it will cleanse from the defilement of false teaching. After reading, pray by yourself or with others.

For a while, you may have difficulty concentrating when reading the Bible and praying because of the trauma you experienced and the bondage you were in. You may even have no desire for Bible reading or prayer right now.

At first you may read with your old cultish "glasses" on. Your former group's pet verses and concepts may still color your thinking and trigger adverse emotional reactions. Even singing certain choruses may do the same.

But keep right on reading anyway. Saturating yourself in God's Word will bring release from bondage and a change in your thinking.

That's what helped Karen, the young, single woman who left our former church. She was so traumatized, she could scarcely function normally. But gradually she found that reading long passages of the Bible at a time gave her a better perspective on the "whole counsel of God." It put verses in their proper context, rather than in isolation. She began seeing that her previous leaders had taken certain Scriptures out of context and twisted their meanings.

Eventually, Karen found that immersing herself in God's Word brought the following benefits:

*Cleansing from sin.* Paul said, "Christ loved the church and gave himself up for her to make her holy, cleansing her by the washing with water through the word" (Eph. 5:25–26).

*Emotional healing.* The psalmist said, "He [God] sent forth his word and healed them" (Ps. 107:20).

*Guidance.* David said, "Your word is a lamp to my feet and a light for my path" (Ps. 119:105).

*Protection from sin.* David said, "How can a young man keep his way pure? By living according to your word" (Ps. 119:9).

*Spiritual food.* Peter said, "Like newborn babies, crave pure spiritual milk, so that by it you may grow up in your salvation" (1 Pet. 2:2). Jesus said to the devil, "Man does not live on bread alone, but on every word that comes from the mouth of God" (Matt. 4:4).

*Spiritual strength.* Paul said to the Ephesian believers, "Now I commit you to God and to the word of his grace, which can build you up" (Acts 20:32).

*Spiritual understanding.* The psalmist prayed, "Open my eyes that I may see wonderful things in your law" (Ps. 119:18). Later, he said, "The unfolding of your words gives light; it gives understanding to the simple" (Ps. 119:130).

*2. Look for another church and attend regularly.* If you have come out of a difficult situation, you may not feel like going to *any* church. The thought of finding another may be more than you can handle. So you stay home.

This may be all right for a time. At first, you'll lick your wounds in private. Yet as healing comes, you need another church home for worship, fellowship, and encouragement.

But "church hunting" takes courage.

Doris, an attractive middle-ager, and her husband were deeply involved in a large cultish sect—she as private secretary to the leader and he as a minister. After years of faithful service, they were stunned when they learned that the leader's son, second in command, was living an immoral life. But that revelation was what it took to get them to leave.

"Sometimes we don't see the real fruit of an individual until we're involved—and that takes time, observation, and evaluation," Doris says today. "No wonder so many people who come out of cultish organizations fear involvement with another group."

A word of caution: Do look for a church that faithfully teaches the Word of God and for a pastor who lives a godly life.

At this point, you may ask how you can tell a true leader

from a false one. Jesus gave a simple guideline—look at his fruit. He said: "Watch out for false prophets. They come to you in sheep's clothing, but inwardly they are ferocious wolves. By their fruit you will recognize them. Do people pick grapes from thornbushes, or figs from thistles?

"Likewise, every good tree bears good fruit, but a bad tree bears bad fruit. A good tree cannot bear bad fruit, and a bad tree cannot bear good fruit. Every tree that does not bear good fruit is cut down and thrown into the fire. Thus, by their fruit you will recognize them" (Matt. 7:15–20).

What fruit will be seen in a false prophet? Again, let's go to the Bible for our answer: "The acts of the sinful nature are obvious: sexual immorality, impurity and debauchery; idolatry and witchcraft; hatred, discord, jealousy, fits of rage, selfish ambition, dissensions, factions and envy; drunkenness, orgies, and the like. I warn you, as I did before, that those who live like this will not inherit the kingdom of God" (Gal. 5:19–21).

The apostle Paul warned Timothy: "If anyone teaches false doctrines and does not agree to the sound instruction of our Lord Jesus Christ and to godly teaching, he is conceited and understands nothing. He has an unhealthy interest in controversies and quarrels about words that result in envy, strife, malicious talk, evil suspicions and constant friction between men of corrupt mind" (1 Tim. 6:3–5).

To the church at Galatia, Paul wrote: "Let us not become conceited, provoking and envying each other" (Gal. 5:26).

The same passage of Scripture gives the fruit borne of a godly leader: "But the fruit of the Spirit is love, joy, peace, patience, kindness, goodness, faithfulness, gentleness and self-control" (Gal. 5:22–23).

Here are some more good fruits: "The wisdom that comes from heaven is first of all pure; then peace-loving, considerate, submissive, full of mercy and good fruit, impartial and sincere" (James 3:17).

Let's list these so we can see them more clearly:

Fruits of a godly leader:

- Consideration of others
- Faithfulness
- Gentleness

- Goodness
- Impartiality
- Joy
- Kindness
- Love
- Mercifulness
- Patience
- Peace
- Purity
- Self-control
- Sincerity
- Submission

Fruits of a False Leader:

- Conceit
- Debauchery
- Discord
- Dissensions
- Drunkenness
- Envy
- Factions
- Fits of rage
- Hatred
- Idolatry
- Impurity
- Jealousy
- Orgies
- Provoking others
- Selfish ambition
- Sexual immorality
- Witchcraft

*3. Seek godly counsel.* You may feel so confused, betrayed, and upset that you need to counsel with a mature Christian. As you pour out your thoughts and feelings and pray with him or her, you may feel relieved. You will find it helpful just to know that someone cares and understands. He or she may have worthwhile insight and advice, also.

*4. Be patient.* Remember, "this too shall pass." The trauma you feel is similar to going through a death or a divorce. You've likely experienced losses of finances, friendships, even family relationships. When added to the betrayal and disillusionment, you've been through a lot. It may take several months, even years, to get over the effects. Don't be discouraged. Remember that time and the Lord's love are great healers.

5. *Give thanks to the Lord.* Jesus tells us: "Blessed are you when men hate you, when they exclude you and insult you and reject your name as evil, because of the Son of Man. Rejoice in that day and leap for joy, because great is your reward in heaven. For that is how their fathers treated the prophets" (Luke 6:22–23).

You may have come out of your group "on a stretcher" from wounds received. The last thing you feel like doing is praising the Lord. But that is exactly what he tells you to do. You are to "leap" for joy, because your reward is great in heaven.

For what should you praise the Lord? First of all, praise him for who he is. Thank him that he is faithful, that he never changes, that he is merciful and compassionate, that he will never fail you.

The psalmist David said, "Great is the Lord and most worthy of praise; his greatness no one can fathom" (Ps. 145:3).

Second, praise the Lord for delivering you. In his goodness, he brought you out of the "house of bondage." You can tell him:

"Lord, I don't feel like praising you, but I choose to praise, anyway. Thank you for delivering me from bondage and deception."

Praise him with other words of your choosing. Praise him in song. Sing along with a music tape or record. Play songs of praise on an instrument. Read psalms of praise aloud. You might even try a few jumps for joy.

The manner in which you praise the Lord doesn't matter— as long as you do it. He tells you to do this for your own good. In praise, you will find healing for your wounded soul and protection from satanic attacks.

After God delivered David from the clutches of King Saul, he said: "He [God] lifted me out of the slimy pit, out of the mud and mire; he set my feet on a rock and gave me a firm place to stand. He put a new song in my mouth, a hymn of praise to our God" (Ps. 40:2–3).

6. *Keep your eyes on the Lord.* The greatest lesson you will

learn from your experience is to keep your eyes on the Lord, not on a leader. Trust him, depend on him, talk often with him. He will never fail you.

The prophet Jeremiah painted a vivid picture of the contrast between trusting people or God: "Cursed is the one who trusts in man, who depends on flesh for his strength and whose heart turns away from the LORD. He will be like a bush in the wastelands; he will not see prosperity when it comes. He will dwell in the parched places of the desert, in a salt land where no one lives.

"But blessed is the man who trusts in the LORD, whose confidence is in him. He will be like a tree planted by the water that sends out its roots by the stream. It does not fear when heat comes; its leaves are always green. It has no worries in a year of drought and never fails to bear fruit" (Jer. 17:5–8).

In warning Christians about aberrant groups, author David Breese says: "One of the marks of a cult is that it elevates the person and the words of a human leader to a messianic level. . . . Too many religiously disposed people are not intellectually responsible enough to think for themselves. Their easy mental acquiescence has led them to seek a leader who can give them all of the answers and personalize or objectify their religious need. They want someone to speak to them with authority, even finality."[7]

An editorial in *Christianity Today* agrees: "Ultimate commitment is safely made only to God. No man or woman can be ultimately trusted. . . . We follow imperfect human leaders because they are the only ones we have. But we do not follow them blindly. We subject their fallible guidance to the perfect and infallible guide God himself has given us in Scripture. In the final analysis we obey God rather than men" (Acts 4:19).[8]

So read your Bible and pray. Attend a Bible-based church regularly. Seek godly counsel. Be patient. Praise God. Keep your eyes him.

If you do these six things, you will get your spiritual boat back into the mainstream of Christianity.

## Questions
1. Why should you praise God for a bad experience?

2.  What can a daily devotional time do for you?
3.  Should you look for another church—even when your previous one failed you? Explain.
4.  How can you tell a true leader from a false one?
5.  What is the value of godly counsel?
6.  Why should you be patient when healing is a lengthy process?
7.  What is the greatest lesson you can learn from a bad experience in an aberrant group?

# Part IV:

# Shiloh:
# A Historical Example

# Chapter 14
# A Community of the Holy

There is no doubt that a community of holy men
and women, desirous of knowing the deepest truths
and entering into partnership for the world's
evangelization, will soon be gathered to this neighborhood.
—Frank Sandford, 1897[1]

At the turn of this century, the "Holy-Ghost-and-Us" Bible
School, later known simply as "Shiloh" or "The Kingdom,"
was the largest institution of its kind. In a rural setting near
Durham, Maine, it covered 1,500 acres and included forty-
four buildings and farms.

We are personally interested in the history of Shiloh
because John's maternal grandparents—T. Albert and Carrie
Field—moved there in 1899, where his mother Elisabeth
Lawless Ham and two aunts were born. Also, all that is left
of Shiloh is located just five miles from Brunswick where
John grew up.

We both lived in Brunswick in the late 1980s, and Agnes
became better acquainted with John's family and other
people who had spent time at Shiloh in their youth or who
knew others who had.

Here's the story of John's grandparents, as related to us:

With a flick of the reins, twenty-nine-year-old T. Albert
("Bert") Field hurried his team of horses along a rough,
country road near Durham, Maine, in the summer of 1899.

He glanced at his young wife Carrie beside him in the wagon. Soft brown curls peeked out from under her sunbonnet brim. Her cheeks flushed a delicate pink, and her blue eyes sparkled with excitement when she smiled back at her husband.

"Happy, honey?" Bert asked.

"I can hardly wait to get there! At last, we've found the group we've been looking for." She smiled at four-year-old Ithiel and two-year-old Ruth sitting beside her.

The horses trotted along the dusty road, through verdant pine woods and past small farms. The young family in the bouncing wagon watched farmers hoeing potatoes and corn under the warm sun. As they rounded a bend, Bert and Carrie caught glimpses through the trees of a golden dome sparkling on a hill.

"There it is!" Carrie cried. "That's Shiloh, children. We're in for a wonderful adventure, aren't we, dear?"

"I hope so," Bert said. "I like Frank Sandford's preaching, and I'm mighty glad he's a good Baptist."

Bert grinned at his excited wife as she chatted on. Deep down, however, he wondered if he had been wise to sell his thriving jewelry store in nearby Brunswick and pull up roots just when he was getting established. Had his training at Tiffany's in New York City been for nothing? Was it sensible to sell their comfortable home and furniture to turn the proceeds over to Frank Sandford and Shiloh? It's a good thing he had given his folks some money to keep for them in case things didn't work out.

But then, Bert thought, living with other Christians sounded wonderful. They would share "all things in common." And Sandford promised to take care of them the rest of their lives with a "social security" and retirement system combined. Guess he would just have to trust God more fully.

Shaking himself, Bert came back to the present in time to hear Carrie say, "And we'll both be able to take classes in the Bible school and get the training we've always wanted. But the part I like best is that we can help take the gospel to the ends of the earth."

The team slowly pulled the loaded wagon up an incline and around another bend. Then the family saw it—three turrets. A seven-storied tower capped with a gold-leaf crown.

Colorful flags whipping in the breeze. Two magnificent "gates of praise" atop a long staircase. Wide verandas wrapped around a 600-foot building. It was reminiscent of a medieval castle ruling a hill.

As the wagon lumbered up the long driveway and stopped, doors opened in the building, and people rushed out to greet the new arrivals. A man held the reins while Bert jumped down, then helped Carrie and the children off the wagon seat. Warm hands grasped theirs. Smiles radiated like sunshine everywhere.

Suddenly, an imposing figure of a man cut a swath through the crowd. Carrying himself confidently, the Reverend Frank Sandford strode forward, his dark mustache topping a wide smile.

"Welcome! Welcome to the kingdom!" He shook their hands with a strong grip. "So glad you've joined us."

After the greetings were over and the milling people returned to their work, Sandford walked Bert and Carrie to a small building off to one side.

On the way, Bert slipped a hand into his inner jacket pocket and drew out an envelope. He handed it to Sandford. "Here's something to help with the work. We sold our house and jewelry business and won't be needing the money now."

"Wonderful! Praise the Lord!" Sandford slapped Bert's shoulder.

"You may as well take the team and wagon, too. We won't be needing them either."

Sandford stopped and ran an appraising eye over the well-groomed chestnut horses and sturdy wagon. Once again, the leader held out his hand to shake Bert's. "God bless you for your generosity, brother. We'll put them to good use."

By this time, they were in front of the small building.

"This is going to be our post office," Sandford explained. "We need someone to serve our growing community as postmaster. With your business background, we think this would be an ideal job for you. Will you take it?"

"Sure. Guess I can learn to handle it."

As they stepped inside the dim interior, Sandford said, "Of course, we'll get this fixed up with a counter, shelves, and whatever else you'll need. You and your family can sleep upstairs." He waved toward a narrow ladder. Another smile, and he was gone.

While Carrie and the children watched, Bert drove the wagon near the door, then carried a load of bedding up the ladder. He promptly knocked his head on the low rafters, for he couldn't stand upright.

After carrying up the rest of their belongings, Bert came down and held the baby while the youngsters clambered up the ladder. His pregnant wife proceeded more slowly. "Watch your head, Carrie," he called.

"Oh, boy! This'll be fun!" Young Ithiel yelled down to his father.

The little wife looked around her new home. She saw a double iron bed, two single cots, and a washstand with enamel basin and pitcher.

"At least, you won't have to worry about cooking up there," Bert called from below. "We'll be eating in the dining hall with the rest of the folks."

Carrie took a deep breath before managing, "Fine." This was a bit different than she had imagined. Would she be able to cope? Could she manage that ladder now that she was pregnant again? Well, she'd just have to take one day at a time. She led the squealing toddlers back down the ladder to begin their new lives.

Bert soon established himself as an important member of Shiloh. As one of the few businessmen, he not only served as postmaster, but also as water commissioner and the appraiser of valuable items donated to the group.

During fund drives open to the public, followers sang rousing hymns while filing forward. They dropped money, wedding rings, brooches, necklaces, watches, and silverware into a large collection plate in front of the pulpit.

All the while, Sandford kept a running total, which he shouted out to the beat of the music.

Bert sat at a table on the platform. His job was to estimate the dollar value of donations. It was a heady time for the young Yankee jeweler. *All this to the glory of God*, he thought, *and the furthering of his kingdom*.

For the first few years, Bert and Carrie were happy in the glow of their "honeymoon" experience at Shiloh. They enjoyed meeting new people and talking about the things of the Lord. The daily services and prayer meetings were stimulating. Sandford and his lovely wife Helen, as well as their new friends, seemed caring and loving.

As time passed, however, the young couple became uncomfortable at Shiloh. Was it just their imagination, or were others feeling the same? Something was wrong, but they weren't sure what. And they didn't dare say a word to anyone else.

The Fields did notice gradual changes, however. Bible classes had turned into lengthy harangues on Sandford's often revolutionary doctrines. They also observed that members considered his words as important as God's.

Equally disturbing were Sandford's abusive actions—his angry confrontations with those who disagreed or questioned his authority. His blithely spending their money on everything from golden harps to yachts instead of food for his hungry followers bothered their Yankee thrift and sense of justice.

Deeply disillusioned, Bert and Carrie left in 1904 under a cloud of rejection from their friends at Shiloh and warnings of judgment from Sandford. In fact, these warnings were so dire that the Fields had a family portrait taken soon after they left. With "tongue-in-cheek," Bert told family and friends, "We want you to have something to remember us by—in case Sandford's judgments come true."

Since they were penniless, except for the money they had left with Bert's parents, something drastic had to be done to raise capital. The senior Fields sold their farm near Durham. Part of the money was used to build a three-story, frame house on upper Pleasant Street in Brunswick. Bert and his family lived upstairs and his parents on the main floor. With the rest of the money, Bert reestablished his jewelry business on Maine Street.

After going through the trauma of leaving Shiloh themselves, they helped others who left. They hid them in their house, barn, or woods from Shilohites who tried to hunt them down. They gave them money to return to their homes and wrote letters of recommendation for those needing jobs.

In May 1905, Field was a witness for the prosecution in a custody case. A grandfather wanted to get his grandson out of Shiloh and be given custody of him. The *Lewiston Saturday Journal* gives this report: "Albert Field, formerly postmaster of Shiloh, testified that he . . . left the place because he felt that he needed a complete rest so he could think for himself. He was exhausted mentally as a consequence of the doubts and questions constantly raised in his mind by Sandford."[2]

The Fields joined the Cumberland Street Freewill Baptist Church, then transferred to the Berean Baptist Church shortly before the two churches merged. Bert was Sunday-school superintendent from 1911 to 1942, nearly thirty-one years. He also served as church treasurer for several years, besides being a deacon. Carrie served as cradle-roll superintendent. They raised ten children.

When T. Albert Field led the Sunday school in singing, "'Tis So Sweet to Trust in Jesus,'" his eyes often filled with tears. He and Carrie had learned by hard experience to trust in Jesus, not in a leader.

### Sandford Began Well

Shiloh's founder, the Reverend Frank W. Sandford, emerged from evangelicalism. He graduated from Bates College in Lewiston, Maine, in 1886, then briefly attended Cobb Divinity School, both Freewill Baptist institutions. He pastored Baptist churches in Topsham, Maine, and Somersworth, New Hampshire, following his ordination.

After meeting Helen Kinney, a former society girl from a wealthy home, he fell in love. She was the first missionary to Japan with the Christian and Missionary Alliance, but he persuaded her to return to marry him. He left the Baptist ministry in 1893 when he became dissatisfied with pastoral work, then traveled as an independent evangelist, holding campaigns in small towns throughout Maine with good results.

Feeling the need for giving his new converts additional teaching, he began a Bible school with five students in a farmhouse near Durham, Maine, in 1896. Charles E. Holland, from the Gordon Missionary Training School (now Gordon-Conwell Theological Seminary) in Boston, Massachusetts, came to be his assistant.

Fueled by his paper *Tongues of Fire* with news of healings, signs, and wonders, flames of this new movement swept across North America and the British Isles. Sandford, a dynamic personage with oratorical gifts, drew followers like candy draws children. He soon attracted whole families from as far away as Washington State and England.

Shiloh grew into a commune of six hundred men and women, besides children. All were earnest Christians, eager to win the world for Christ in their generation.

In studying Shiloh and its leader, we noticed certain cult-like characteristics: charisma and pride, anger when questioned, greed, an authoritarian structure, exclusivity, the demand for loyalty and honor, and a reliance on "new revelation." Indeed, Shiloh and Sandford composed a historical microcosm of aberrant Christianity.

## Charisma and Pride

Frank Sandford had three characteristics of a born leader— penetrating eyes, persuasive speech, and a dynamic personality.

Along with piercing blue eyes, he was a handsome man with fair hair, a neatly trimmed beard, and a clear complexion. An athletic build filled out broad shoulders, emphasizing his lean hips and strong-cut jaw.[3]

Sandford also was an eloquent speaker. Arnold White, whose family moved to Shiloh when he was a teenager, says that Sandford "impressed me favorably—a preacher one could listen to without boredom." With "a laugh that shot up like a geyser," he was so confident while preaching that White felt he was "a man who knew what he was talking about."[4]

Even more, Sandford had that certain something, that charisma that drew people to him and made them feel he was someone special. At the height of his career, one follower described his magnetism as a "special heavenly tingle that accompanied [him] wherever he went." His coming into a gathering spread a "breathless thrill" through those who loved him, conveying a sense of "safety and comfort."[5]

Flushed with success and the adulation of his people, Sandford first called himself "the representative of God," a "prophet," an "apostle," the "shepherd David," and finally "Elijah" sent to prepare the world for Christ's coming reign. His partner, C. E. Holland, was "Moses." He felt they were the "two witnesses" who would prophesy for 1,260 days in the end times. If anyone tries to harm them, "fire comes from their mouths and devours their enemies" (Rev. 11:3, 5).

## Anger and Intimidation

Not only did Sandford grow proud, but he also was angry with anyone who questioned or disagreed with him. Stormy confrontations became his way of life.

Although such scoldings were done in private at first, more and more of them took place in public. Even his gentle wife Helen could not escape his reprimands from the pulpit. Once he slapped her face on the platform in the middle of an angry outburst. On another occasion, he ordered all his assistant "ministers" off the platform and threw their chairs after them while shouting judgments upon them.[6]

One time Sandford's anger even resulted in death. Teenager Leander Bartlett and a friend decided to run away from Shiloh to find work. When young Bartlett contracted diptheria, the leader called him "rebellious" and said he didn't care if he saw Leander's "dead body lying out" before him. He deprived the boy of medical care or prayers for healing. Eight days later, Leander died.[7]

Most of his people, amazingly, quietly accepted his angry rebukes as from God. Former member Arnold White explains that they were so confident their leader's "moods and words were God-inspired," that they accepted his rebukes "as necessary to the purifying" of their souls. To defend themselves "was unthinkable," since to do so "might intimate error on the part" of their trusted leader.[8]

## Greed and Fraud

As time went by, Sandford not only became a proud and angry man, but he also grew greedy. He went beyond teaching his people the importance of giving; he linked such contributions with salvation. "Giving money is one of the ways in which a man keeps saved," he said. "The 'root of all evil,' when it is rooted out, becomes a means of salvation. It is really dangerous not to give."[9]

Sandford urged his followers to sell their homes, land, and possessions, then turn the assets over to him when they moved to Shiloh. After they arrived, he pressured them into giving up all cash and valuables, even stamps and post cards. He pronounced "awful judgments on all who dared to rob God."[10]

Sandford then used the money to finance his grandiose visions and to live comfortably with his family in a separate house from the dormitories. He kept adding to the complex of buildings with the free labor of his followers.

Dreaming of "conquering" all nations with his teaching, he bought a luxurious yacht and a large brigantine sailing vessel for taking worldwide "missionary" cruises. He took along members of the Shiloh band to play as they traveled and even bought two full-sized, golden harps, since he was "David, the sweet singer of Israel."

Meanwhile, the people of the commune suffered constant hunger. "Food was very scarce," former member Estella Sheller said, "even for the men who were laboring day and night on the building." Many days they had only "a light breakfast." Sandford and his family, however, ate well with their own cook to prepare their meals—even on shipboard.[11]

## Enslaving Authoritarian Structure

Shiloh developed an authoritarian structure under Sandford's leadership. With himself on top of the pyramid, he placed the placid Charles Holland directly under him, then a series of various leaders under Holland. Soon everyone had people over them to direct their lives.

As former member Nathan Harriman explained, Sandford taught the theory of "divine authority": that "all authority proceeded from God the Father to Christ the Son," from Christ to his "appointed servant" on earth [Sandford], and "through him to the ministers," and down to the "least of the whole community." Any who disobeyed the leaders disobeyed God himself, Sandford claimed.[12]

## Exclusivity

Early in his ministry, Sandford claimed God said to him, "New wine, new bottles."

"What do you mean, Lord? Do you mean that you want this work to have nothing to do with the labors of others?"

Although he received no reply, "the answer hung in the air." He felt that God implied by silence, "That is exactly what I mean." From then on, he left other groups "severely alone."[13]

So like other cultish groups before and since, Shiloh gradually became a closed community. Members had no contact with other Christians in the area, much less with the general public. In fact, Sandford would not allow them to read newspapers or magazines from the outside.

Isolation developed into an elitist mentality. A former member said Sandford claimed that "his movement represented the last move of God for this age" and that "the rider on the white horse, the opening of the first seal (Rev. 6) represented his work."[14]

The natural result of such elitism and isolation was broken

family ties. Young people at Shiloh wrote enthusiastic letters home about the "new truths" they were learning, such as Sandford being "Elijah" to prepare the way for Christ's coming.

Alarmed, parents pleaded with their children to leave. The young people refused, choosing to remain loyal to their leader. Urged by Sandford, they cut off all contact with their parents and prepared to give themselves to this new movement for life. He taught them to be "so secret" that family members outside the group couldn't learn what was going on inside.[15]

The knife of elitism sliced through the Nathan Harriman family. After three years in leadership, he, his wife, and some of their children left Shiloh. One son and daughter—Joseph and Flora—chose to stay. True to their leader, they had nothing to do with the rest of their family from then on.

Joseph and his twenty-four-year-old sister Flora soon sailed for Jerusalem with a party from Shiloh. The parents heard nothing from them. In August 1906, the Harrimans received a telegram saying, "Flora is gone," with no details. Later, they heard that she had died of a serious disease. But Joseph still maintained his silence.[16]

Sandford's teachings sometimes broke marriage relationships. For instance, the Adamson family was separated when the wife could no longer stand the strain of the strange life in the commune. She took half the children and left for nearby Brunswick. At first, her husband chopped wood and hauled water for her. But Sandford convinced him that since she had "incurred God's displeasure," he should have nothing more to do with her.[17]

## Demanded Loyalty and Honor

Like most aberrant leaders, Sandford demanded blind loyalty from his followers. When he was tried in court for alleged manslaughter and child abuse, a number of disillusioned people left the commune.

As a result, Sandford called members living on and off the grounds for a convention to stem the outgoing tide in the spring of 1904. The climax of the convention came when all members signed a pledge of loyalty on a ten-foot scroll, part of which stated: "I believe . . . in the prophet-prince-priest who is to prepare the Kingdom for the Christ; I believe

in the man who as prophet is called in the Bible 'Elijah'—
and as a prince is called 'David,' and as a priest is called . . .
'The Branch.' I believe that F. W. Sandford of Shiloh, Maine,
USA, tells the truth when he makes proclamation that God
said to him, 'Elijah is here. Testify,' and again, 'I have found
David,' words spoken as applying to himself personally. I
believe in and accept him as such."[18]

## "New" Extrabiblical Revelation

Sandford taught the major tenets of the faith until he began
listening to and relying upon a "voice" which he thought
was God's. His teaching gradually became aberrant.

For instance, he taught baptismal regeneration and that
all followers had to be baptized or rebaptized by him. He
also taught British Israelism, believing that Great Britain and
the United States were the true Israel. All the promises in
Scripture concerning the Jews applied to them.

Sandford also taught an extreme form of healing. Members
were not allowed to receive medical help from doctors,
nurses, or hospitals. Nor were they to take any medications.
Since it was always God's will to heal, they were to look to
him alone.

Moreover, Sandford made false predictions, such as "a
great earthquake and tidal wave two hundred feet high"
would sweep across Maine. "Shooting stars will destroy
whole villages," he shouted. "Then and then only will people
flock to our hilltop to be with God's chosen people. Shiloh
will become the greatest city in the world."[19]

## The Kingdom Crumbles

Standing on a dock in Portland, Maine, Dr. Stuart gazed
at a slanting rain striking the gray Atlantic Ocean. He
shivered and pulled up the collar of his black raincoat.

Quarantine doctor Albert S. Stuart had been told to expect
a troubled ship on this Saturday, October 21, 1911, but he
was not given its name or description.

He watched a schooner inch its way into Portland Harbor.
It was battered, covered with barnacles, shrouded with sea
grass. Its torn sails and broken spars gave mute evidence of
battles with hurricanes. Gaunt, bearded seamen lined the
rail, looking hungrily at the rocky beaches and low skyline
of their home port. Brilliant autumn foliage in reds, oranges,

and yellows surrounded by dark-green pines, stood out in sharp contrast to the otherwise gray scene.

The mysterious ship anchored near the quarantine station and hoisted a yellow flag, signaling the need for medical help.

Rushing into his office, Dr. Stuart grabbed his black bag and ordered his associates to bring medical supplies. Then he, his medics, and immigration inspector Timothy Eliot boarded the ship. They found fifty-seven starving people, some lying on bunks, too ill to move.

"Get Banks here immediately!" Stuart ordered an assistant. He knew Dr. Charles E. Banks, ranking port physician, needed to make an inspection of this disaster.

Dr. Banks hurried to the dock with horse and buggy. When he examined the patients below deck, he found loose teeth, bleeding gums, open wounds, and severe anemia. Many looked like living skeletons.[20]

The once-splendid yacht was the *Coronet*, former pride of the New York Yacht Club and built by a millionaire. Now it belonged to the Reverend Frank Sandford and Holy-Ghost-and-Us Society, better known as Shiloh.

Former member Helga Adamson heard that state authorities had put her son John in a hospital in Portland. Rushing to the scene, she wept over his once-sturdy body wasted by starvation and scurvy. She prayed for him, holding a scrawny hand and willing her strength into him. But it was too late. Nineteen-year-old John died ten days after reaching home port.[21]

What went wrong on this tragic voyage? Why was this ship in the North Atlantic during hurricane season? With so many sick and dying on board, why didn't it make for port sooner?

To find the answers to these questions, we must trace the journey from its beginning.

Months earlier, former member Florence Whittaker sued Sandford for $100,000 for forcible detention when she had tried to leave the group.[22]

To escape the law, Sandford took to sea on the *Coronet* on June 1, 1910. With him were his wife Helen and their five young children. Twenty-three other Shiloh members went along, some as crew. The *Kingdom*, the group's brigantine, soon joined them.

After cruising the coastal waters for seven months, the

ships sailed across the Atlantic. The lumbering brigantine tried to follow the yacht up the Gambia River on the northwestern African coast. Not having proper charts, the ship ran aground and became a total loss. Sandford ordered it set afire as a "burnt offering" for Africa. Its thirty-six passengers and crew members crowded onto the yacht.

Six weeks later, it began its return journey. The vessel leaked so badly that the crew kept busy pumping. Even though they bought provisions from passing steamers occasionally, they were down to one meal a day—often cornmeal mush or fish soup.

A month later, they reached the coast of Venezuela. But Sandford insisted that they make no stops and head north to pray for Greenland. God had forbidden him to visit the continents over which he had prayed the year before, he said, including North and South America.

By then, scurvy was taking its toll. Two middle-aged men and a two-year-old girl died.

On September 6, as the yacht sailed past Newfoundland, two crew members asked that the ship head for home.

Gathering the people together, Sandford said, "I'll not use duress on anyone. We'll turn around, as these men have asked, but I'll add a solemn warning: God spoke this word to me—'distress.' Reflect well on what you are doing."[23]

George McKay savored each spoonful of his bean soup for breakfast. He knew he would get nothing more except a little popcorn for supper. He looked at the other crewmen, thin and ill with scurvy, slowly starving to death. "Oh, God, have mercy," he prayed.

McKay scanned the forecastle awash with sea water. It was built for ten people, but twice that number were here— two men to a bunk. The stench was terrible, for the plumbing no longer worked. They couldn't open portholes for fresh air, with heavy seas breaking over the vessel.

George Hughey, a resourceful fisherman, felt miserably ill. He went to Sandford and asked, "Will you please pray for my healing?"

"No!" the leader growled. "You refused to come under my divine authority recently, so God is dealing with you."

Two days later, "Uncle George" died. The group held a brief service and slipped his body overboard.[24]

After receiving slim supplies from a passing freighter,

Sandford called crew and passengers downstairs to the saloon. "You ought to thank the Lord that my family is aboard," he said. "If it had not been for us, none of you would have got provisions. God has let me know that we are a holy family."

Unfortunately, crew members saw none of the provisions.

During the next month, the battered yacht encountered four major storms, one after the other. With strong headwinds against them, they took three weeks to cover what usually took three days.

The crewmen lived and slept in wet clothes, too weak and ill to care. They had unmistakable signs of scurvy—bleeding gums, loosening teeth, ugly boils, and bowel miseries.[25]

On October 16, Ralph Merrill and Charles Hughey, George's brother, both died.[26] Two days later, Stuart Wolfe followed. The remaining men were so weak that it took six of them to carry one emaciated body up on deck, sew it in canvas, weight it with ballast, and lower it over the side.[27] Nine bodies were thus committed to the deep during the voyage. Two more died after a few days on shore, making a total of eleven deaths.

With broken masts, shredded sails, and open seams, the twenty-five-year-old schooner limped into Portland Harbor seventeen months from its departure.

Frank Sandford had been free from the law on the high seas. But it was waiting for him when he reached land. Deputy Sheriff Arthur Fickett boarded the ship. He found Sandford and served him Florence Whittaker's writ for forcible detention. He was released on bail.

But authorities knew nothing of the deaths at sea. When this came to light, Deputy US Marshall Fred E. Stevens searched Shiloh and arrested the leader.

Sandford was charged with the death of Charles Hughey by not providing adequate provisions or taking him to port. Assistant District Attorney Arthur Chapman did not mention the other deaths in his warrant at this time.[28]

Since this second arrest occurred too late in the day for the $10,000 bail to be arranged, Sandford spent the night in jail.

The next day, two elderly ladies provided the needed money. Eighty-seven-year-old Mrs. C. A. Hallett told a reporter, "I have absolute faith in Mr. Sandford. Before entering Shiloh, I did not think it possible for a man to be perfect, but I have learned that there is one perfect man. Mr. Sandford is perfect; he is honest and absolutely sincere in his life."[29]

Sandford's trial began December 8 in the US District Court in Portland. The leader pleaded not guilty.

Crewman Roland Whittom witnessed that Sandford taught that he was "Elijah," the forerunner of Christ's second coming. He expected to be treated and obeyed like Jesus Christ. Disobedience was punished by disfellowshiping or worse.[30]

Since he refused counsel, Sandford spoke for himself from the witness stand. Dressed in a neat, black suit, he looked like a prosperous businessman. His gray hair and long beard made him appear older than his forty-nine years.

In his defense, Sandford stressed that the original group on the *Coronet* had planned to go to Greenland from the beginning. This destination was unchanged by the wreck of the *Kingdom*. When he went to God for guidance, he asked, "Father, what next, now that we have this company on board?"

He said he received the answer, "Continue."

The original thirty on the yacht were absolutely obedient to the will of God, living in "the white light of eternity." Those from the wrecked vessel, however, brought a spirit of discontent, he alleged.

For an hour and fifteen minutes, Sandford testified on his own behalf. Sometimes he spoke in a low voice, his words scarcely audible. At other times, he shouted, slapping the rail of the witness stand. Occasionally his voice broke in a half-sob. From beginning to end, he protested that he had done everything at the command of God.

The jury returned its verdict—guilty. That single word shattered the silence into a thousand murmurs throughout the courtroom.[31]

On his last day of freedom, Sunday, December 17, the leader preached a ten-hour farewell address to his six hundred followers at Shiloh. "I am the chosen one of God!" he shouted from his gilded pulpit. "The whole world will fall at my feet!"[32]

The next morning, Sandford was sentenced to ten years in the US penitentiary in Atlanta, Georgia. With tear-dimmed eyes and quivering hands, he fumbled for his cap, then walked slowly out of the courtroom unattended.[33]

That night, "Elijah II" boarded a train with two deputy marshalls and two robbers. He was dressed in a smart blue suit and wore a sailing cap bearing his insignia as commodore of the Kingdom Yacht Club.[34]

Two days later, the iron gates of the penitentiary clanged behind him.

On September 6, 1918, after seven years, Sandford was released for good behavior.

The joyful reunion at Shiloh was mixed with grief. He found his wife "wrinkled and atremble with shattered nerves." Two of his teenage daughters had run away. In the face of dire hunger and abject poverty, the commune's farms had been mortgaged. The fires of faith in Sandford and his teaching burned low in the hearts of many.[35]

Disappointed, Sandford took his family and moved to Boston. He gradually drew those "true" to him, especially young people.[36]

In February 1920, "The Scattering" occurred. Sandford sent a message to those still on the hilltop—"Work!" Most left "the kingdom" at Shiloh, getting jobs in their home towns or elsewhere. Several single ladies and widows moved to a group home in Boston.

The breakup of the commune was furthered by fresh government investigations and lawsuits. Relatives of crew members who died as a result of the last voyage in 1911 wrote Sandford, threatening the renewal of indictments and more jail time. Newspaper reporters hounded him.

Soon the voice he depended on again said to Sandford, "Retire." He took this to mean that "he should vanish, not only from the public, but from his own dear people." He therefore spent the next twenty-eight years hiding in the country. Only a chosen few knew his whereabouts.[37]

He died on March 2, 1948, in Boston.

The deteriorating wooden structure at Shiloh finally was torn down, except for the original building. It still stands in Durham, Maine, and is used for Sunday services.

Other followers moved to new headquarters called "Fairwood," built in 1951 on Old Marlborough Road outside Dublin, New Hampshire. Its Kingdom Press continues to publish Sandford's sermons and writings, which are used by the few students in Fairwood Bible Institute.

In spite of unfulfilled prophecies, these followers still

believe in Frank W. Sandford. As one says, "Until we find some prophet who lives closer to God, we will stay loyal to this one, convinced that in the light of eternity, we shall see that Frank W. Sandford was indeed a servant of Jehovah, and that the word of God in his mouth was truth."[38]

## Questions

1. Describe Shiloh briefly, giving its purpose.
2. Describe Frank Sandford's background.
3. What cult-like characteristics can be seen in a study of Shiloh and its leader?
4. Describe the last voyage. Why was this ship in the North Atlantic during hurricane season? Why did most deaths occur?
5. Why was Sandford sent to prison?
6. What happened when he was released?

# Appendix

### Historical Drift
Today we have a proliferation of Christian groups similar to Shiloh that have gradually drifted from the moorings of orthodoxy. What historical currents have pushed them in this direction?

### Metaphysical Healing Movement
In the late 1800s, three religious systems grew out of a renewed interest in positive mental attitudes, healing, and prosperity. They were New Thought, Christian Science, and Unity. Composing the metaphysical healing movement, they all flowed from one source—the writings of a Maine clockmaker, Phineas P. Quimby.

*New Thought*
Phineas Parkhurst Quimby (1802-1866), born in Lebanon, New Hampshire, became seriously ill with tuberculosis.

Quimby had a sick friend who claimed he had cured himself by riding horseback. Since Quimby was too weak to do the same, he tried riding in his carriage as fast as the horse would go. He claimed he arrived home totally well.

This experience led Quimby to adopt a "mind-over-matter" or "mental-healing" philosophy. He became convinced that disease was nothing more than an error of the mind.[1]

Other factors influenced Quimby's thinking, too, and their

roots reached back to the previous century. Between 1774 and 1814, German physician Franz Anton Mesmer discovered the "powers of the subconscious mind" which he attributed to magnetism. Later, he said this power was a fluid emanating from the healer to the patient.

In 1784, Count Maxime de Puysegur discovered that Mesmer's alleged "magnetic fluid" actually was the power of the mind. With this discovery came the introduction of hypnotism and somnambulism.

In 1836, French hypnotist Charles Poyen introduced "mesmerism" to New England. Quimby heard him lecture at Belfast, Maine. Poyen told Quimby afterwards that the latter possessed "vast psychic power." Quimby, now a Belfast clock-maker, tried hypnotism on sick people with surprising success. In 1859, his growing practice led him to move to larger quarters at the International Hotel in Portland, Maine.

Over a period of time, Quimby developed a philosophy of what he termed "New Thought" or "Christian Science." He had such success in healing people through "mind-over-matter" that many proclaimed him "the pioneer mental healer" of his day. Although he never published, he did commit his teachings and practices to ten volumes of longhand manuscripts and freely lent them to his patients and disciples.[2]

We may summarize Quimby's revolutionary New Thought theology as follows:

1. *Revelation knowledge.* "Revelation knowledge" is divinely inspired to one's spirit and bypasses the mind and body. "Sense knowledge," on the other hand, is obtained through the intellect and five senses.

2. *Identification with God.* Jesus' death on the cross did not atone for our sins. Rather, he took man's satanic nature and was "reborn" in hell. Identified with him, believers can become deified and incarnations of God.

3. *Faith and positive confession.* Faith is "infinite power" governed by "great immutable laws and forces that run through all the universe."[3] It is the "drawing power of the mind" which confesses the unseen into the seen. Through faith, man has creative power.[4]

4. *Healing.* Quimby taught that "disease is what follows the disturbance of the mind or spiritual matter . . . . It is mind diverted by error, and Truth is the destruction of this

opinion."[5] All sickness, then, is the result of unbelief and sin. Negative thoughts and words cause disease and can infect others. One should deny physical symptoms and not seek medical help.

5. *Prosperity.* Faith is the "law of success" which gives one the ability to prosper financially. This law is triggered by positive thinking and confession.[6] Early New Thought teachers "attributed their ability to acquire riches to psychic and occultic power," such as visualization.[7]

Quimby's New Thought theories spread quickly. His followers spawned two other major metaphysical religious systems: Christian Science and Unity. Not surprisingly, their beliefs and vocabulary are similar.

### Christian Science

Mary Baker Eddy (1821-1910) was born in Bow, New Hampshire. Raised by strict Congregationalist parents, she reacted against their beliefs at a young age. She had convulsions and a severe spinal disease during her early years.[8]

Baker's marital life turned out to be as troubling as her physical condition. In 1843, she married businessman George Washington Glover. He died the next year of yellow fever. A few months later, she gave birth to their son George. These events so affected her mentally and emotionally that she was forced to send young George to live with relatives.

Mrs. Glover married dentist Daniel M. Patterson in 1853. Because of her physical and emotional problems, he left her thirteen years later. She obtained a divorce in 1873. At the age of fifty-six in 1877, Mrs. Patterson married her third husband, Asa Gilbert Eddy, a sewing-machine salesman.

In 1862, Eddy (then Mrs. Patterson) sought help for her illness from "Dr." Quimby in Portland, Maine. She discussed his teachings and methods with him, copied his manuscripts, and observed his treatment of patients.[9] She soon claimed complete healing. In gratitude, she wrote a poem, "To P. P. Quimby, Who Heals the Sick as Jesus Did."[10]

In 1866, shortly after Quimby's death, Eddy fell on an icy sidewalk and injured her back. She claimed doctors gave her only three days to live, but she again was "miraculously cured" by combining Quimby's mental-healing methods with reading the story of Jesus healing the palsied man. From then on, she felt commissioned to spread this "new discovery."

Eddy published her book *Science and Health with Key to the Scriptures* in 1875 and, like Quimby, called her teachings "Christian Science." Critics contend that she plagiarized Quimby's manuscripts after his death. In reply, she denounced him and claimed her teachings came by "divine revelation."[11]

In 1879, Eddy organized the Church of Christ Scientist in Charlestown, Massachusetts. She changed the name in 1892 to the First Church of Christ Scientist.[12]

With some differences, Eddy's theology rests on the cardinal beliefs of Quimby's New Thought:

*1. Revelation knowledge.* Eddy defines knowledge as "evidence obtained from the five corporeal [physical] senses," which "is not divine and is the origin of sin, sickness, and death." It is "the opposite of spiritual Truth and understanding."[13]

*2. Identification with God.* Eddy denied that Christ's death on the cross atoned for sin. She said, "The material blood of Jesus was no more efficacious to cleanse from sin, when it was shed upon 'the accursed tree' than when it was flowing in His veins."[14]

Identified with God, "man is without beginning or end—changeless—THE SAME YESTERDAY AND TODAY AND FOREVER [her emphasis]. All that constitutes man 'is, not shall be,' perfect and complete. All his qualities, faculties, and attributes are spiritual, and immortal, now."[15] "The great spiritual fact must be brought out," she said, "that man is, not shall be, perfect and immortal."[16]

*3. Faith, Positive Confession, and Healing.* Since Eddy rejected the reality of the physical body, she denied physical symptoms. To her, they were an "illusion" and an "error" to be overcome by mental affirmations. She taught: "When the illusion of sickness or sin tempts you, cling steadfastly to God and His idea. Allow nothing but His likeness to abide in your thought. Let neither fear nor doubt overshadow your clear sense and calm trust."[17] She added, "When the first symptoms of disease appear, dispute the testimony of the material senses with divine Science."[18]

Christian Science claims previously unrevealed truth. Eddy's revelations, she affirmed, were "higher" than the

Bible. To her, God was "Divine Principle" and "Immortal Mind." She denied the Trinity, the deity of Jesus Christ, his atoning work on the cross for man's salvation, the existence of sin, sickness, death, heaven, and hell.[19]

Mary Baker Eddy's Christian Science has influenced many other groups, notably the Unity School of Christianity.

## Unity School of Christianity

Ten years after the start of Christian Science, Charles and Myrtle Fillmore founded the Unity School of Christianity.

Charles Sherlock Fillmore (1854-1948) was born near St. Cloud, Minnesota. He married Mary ("Myrtle") Caroline Page in 1881. Raised in New England, Myrtle Fillmore grew up in the Methodist denomination.

The Fillmores established a real-estate business in Kansas City, Missouri, after their marriage. When Myrtle contracted both tuberculosis and malaria, her doctor gave her only six months to live. Charles, too, suffered from a withered leg.

One evening in 1886, the Fillmores attended a lecture. The speaker, E. B. Weeks, said, "I am a child of God, and therefore I do not inherit sickness." Myrtle believed and repeated this statement until she was allegedly healed.

At first, Charles was dubious, but he agreed to study the "science of the mind." He also studied Eastern religions, especially Hinduism and Buddhism. Finally he tried his wife's New-Thought techniques and claimed healing of his withered leg.

Enthused, the Fillmores put together a "new religious system" with heavy borrowings from New Thought and Christian Science. They added their own interpretations, plus Eastern concepts, such as yoga, vegetarianism, and reincarnation, as well as occultism. They changed the name of their religion several times: Modern Thought (1889), Christian Science Thought (1890), Thought (1891), and Unity (1895). Because of its strong publication program, it grew rapidly.

In the belief system of Unity, we can trace New Thought and Christian Science tenets:

1. *Revelation knowledge.* The basis for this belief is ancient gnosticism, the separation of the spirit from the material. The material world is evil, and the spiritual world is good. Only a select few can obtain the secret of this knowledge.[20]

2. *Identification with God.* Like gnosticism, Unity teaches man's ultimate goal is "identification" or deification, achieving "oneness" with God. "We can," the Fillmores wrote, "through Jesus Christ, our Redeemer and example, bring forth the Christ within us, the true self of all is perfect."[21]

Since Unity is a pantheistic system, it believes in an impersonal God and denies the Trinity and the deity of Christ. Anyone can attain Jesus' perfection, it says, by gaining dominion over his thoughts. Man can reach such intimate communication with God that reading the Bible becomes unnecessary.

Jesus' death on the cross to take away sin was unnecessary since "there is no sin, sickness, or death." Salvation involves reincarnation.[22]

3. *Faith and positive confession.* "What we think," wrote Charles Fillmore, "we usually express in words; and our words bring about in our life and affairs what we put into them."[23] Unity leader H. Emile Cady wrote, "[Man] has the power of creating, of bringing into visible form that which before did not exist."[24]

4. *Healing.* Like Christian Science and New Thought, Unity stresses mental healing. However, contrary to Christian Science, Unity contends that matter is not an illusion, but is real. Sin, sickness, and death are also real, although people can overcome them through positive thinking and confession.

5. *Prosperity.* Another major tenet of Unity is material happiness and financial prosperity. No one need be poor. In his book *Prosperity*, Charles Fillmore rewrote the Twenty-third Psalm to say, "The Lord is my banker, my credit is good. . . . Thou fillest my wallet with plenty; my measure runneth over. Surely, goodness and plenty will follow me all the days of my life."[25]

None of these metaphysical healing religions would have made much impact on the evangelical community were it not for one man. He took the "best" of these teaching streams and diverted them into the river of orthodox Christian theology. The result is a flood of polluted water that has spread quickly over some Christian television programs, churches, and schools worldwide. It threatens to engulf them.

## E. W. Kenyon (1867-1948)

The man to whom we refer is Essek William Kenyon. Born in upstate New York, he apparently had a Christian upbringing and a desire to serve Christ. He preached his first sermon in a Methodist church at age nineteen.

Yet the then-popular metaphysical cults intrigued Kenyon. In 1891, he attended the Emerson School of Oratory in Boston, Massachusetts. The school was devoted to New Thought metaphysics, and its founder later became a Christian Scientist. While in Boston, Kenyon attended a Unitarian church, and he studied the works of Ralph Waldo Emerson and New England Transcendentalism.

Kenyon, however, maintained most of his orthodox beliefs. At the turn of the century, he founded Dudley Bible Institute (later Bethel Bible Institute) in Dudley, Massachusetts, and served as president for a number of years. After he left, the school was moved to Providence, Rhode Island.

In 1923, Kenyon moved to Los Angeles, California, where he founded Figueroa Independent Baptist Church and began a daily radio broadcast. After moving to Seattle, Washington, in 1931, he conducted a daily radio program, "Kenyon's Church of the Air." There he founded a church which eventually became New Covenant Baptist Church.

Later, Kenyon devoted most of his time to writing and producing sixteen books and Bible studies. He believed that the metaphysical healing movement had much to offer and admitted to friends that he "freely drew the water of his thinking from the [metaphysical] well." Like New Thought, Christian Science, and Unity, he stressed revelation knowledge, identification with God, positive confession, healing, and financial prosperity.

Although he was not a Pentecostal, his writings greatly influenced leaders in several important Pentecostal movements: the post-World War II healing revival, the Latter-Rain movement, the charismatic renewal, the shepherding movement, and the faith movement. The latter in particular has drawn heavily from his teachings.[26]

## Utopian Communities

While the metaphysical healing movement was developing in the mid-1700s and 1800s, several Utopian communities emerged in the northeastern part of the United States.

One of the earliest was the Shakers, brought to America from England in 1774 by "Mother" Ann Lee. Their first settlement was in Watervliet, New York. Another well-known group was the Oneida Community founded in 1848 in Oneida, New York, by John Humphrey Noyes. Others were the Harmony Society and the Hutterites.

In 1900, faith healer John Alexander Dowie founded Zion City near Chicago, Illinois, which grew to a population of six thousand people. Dowie claimed to be "Elijah, the restorer," the first apostle of a renewed end-times church.

Shiloh was another such community founded at the end of the nineteenth century and was a classic example.

Though short-lived, these Utopian communities were typical of man's attempt to produce a "heaven on earth." They each had "a high degree of social cohesiveness and shared belief." Typically, they were led by dynamic leaders who demanded total obedience to their rules and teachings. Members sacrificed their personal needs and goals to the good of the group.[27]

## Post-World War II Healing Movement

For lack of space, we will not discuss all the evangelists who took part in the post-World War II healing revival, but we will look at two who had profound impacts on modern movements.

### Franklin Hall

Growing up in rural poverty, Franklin Hall had a hunger for God. "I used to pray quite a bit as a boy," he said. "I asked the Lord to give me a new ministry—different from anyone else—a ministry like Elijah."

As an adult, he left the Methodist church and traveled as an independent evangelist during the Great Depression and World War II.[28]

Hall published a book in 1946 that had far-reaching effects, *Atomic Power with God Through Prayer and Fasting.* He gave detailed information on his methods of fasting as the secret of spiritual restoration. Gordon Lindsay's publication *Voice of Healing* and Thomas and Evelyn Wyatt's worldwide radio broadcasts helped spread this message.[29]

From then on, Hall claimed, the major healing evangelists of this period followed his fasting and prayer program with an increase of miracles in their services.

Evangelist Thelma Chaney joined forces with Hall for a time. His results were amazing, she said. "Multitudes fasted. Many in our meetings fasted ten, twenty, thirty and forty days. Miracles, signs and wonders followed."[30]

Hall formed his Deliverance Foundation in 1956 with headquarters in Phoenix, Arizona, where he trained and licensed preachers.

In 1965, he began publishing *Miracle Word* magazine which eventually reached twenty-four thousand subscribers. He distributed a million of his tracts.

By 1970, his foundation had thirty-two affiliated churches and two thousand members. He felt his work would continue to grow. In 1972, he said: "This is going to cover the whole world. It is a stone ministry that is going to grow and become a mountain. . . . Ministers are coming out everywhere. The youth want something for thrills, for kicks, for the body. That's why they go to drugs. . . . We have the answer."[31]

Hall held himself aloof from denominations and from other healing evangelists. The gap between them widened through the years as his theology became deviant.

His "body-felt salvation" theory became the focus of his message. Declaring it was 700 percent "greater than ordinary healing power," he explained that it was "the Holy Ghost fire" warming the body as healing took place. "If we could get it all over them," he said, it would free believers from "sickness, tiredness, odor" and all human frailties. It took "about thirty days to get this established and concentrated all over" the bodies of believers "so that they can live completely above all tiredness and all sickness." His wife, for instance, "had no sickness in eighteen years" and "no tiredness in fifteen years."

This "body-felt salvation" even resulted in no body odor, Hall claimed. Follower Thelma Moore of San Francisco tried the theory out. For six months, she wore the same hose without washing them. "They never did get stiff, . . ." she said. "They never had any unpleasant odor about them."[32] His teaching even raised believers' hopes of "eternal life in a physical body now and a return to life of dead saints."[33]

Hall urged his audiences to sit with "heads up and eyes

open," which would give them "400 percent greater faith." If they raised their right hands and said, "Hello, Jesus," the "Holy Ghost fire" would descend on them. If they raised their left hands, they could smell "the fragrance of Jesus." Hall assured them their dogs would smell a difference on them. This fragrance would permeate their houses and make them "bug proof." They would be "Holy Ghost exterminators."[34]

In his book, he says, "This study teaches one the power and secrets of space flight, space flotation and hovering ability. It gives the Bible formula for weightlessness, the 'raising up' power of those who come to Immortality."[35]

Hall further claimed that those believers who attended his meetings reflected an "Immortal Substance," a "sparkling shining FINE GOLD and SILVER . . . seen on their SKIN, brought about through the faith-power of impartation" [his emphasis].[36]

Franklin Hall is important because of the impact his writings had on healing evangelists to come after him, as well as on leaders of the Latter-Rain movement.

### William Marrion Branham (1909-65)

Greatly influenced by the writings of Franklin Hall and E. W. Kenyon, evangelist William Branham was the "initiator of the post-World War II healing revival."[37]

Branham was born to a poor, alcholic father and a teenage mother in the hills of Kentucky in a dirt-floor log cabin. When the midwife opened the shutters to let in the early-morning sunlight, she claimed she saw a halo about a foot in diameter above the newborn's head.

At age three, he first heard "the voice." At age seven, the voice told him, "Don't you never [sic] drink, smoke, or defile your body in any way. There'll be work for you to do when you get older."[38]

In 1946, this voice finally revealed itself as an "angel." As Branham later told audiences:

> Then along in the night, at about the eleventh hour I had quit praying and was sitting up when I noticed a light flickering in the room. . . . As the light was spreading, . . . I looked up [and] there hung the great star. However, it did not have five points like a star, but looked more like a

ball of fire or light shining down upon the floor. Just then I heard someone walking across the floor, which startled me again . . . . He appeared to be a man who, in human weight, would weigh about two hundred pounds, clothed in a white robe. He had a smooth face, no beard, dark hair down to his shoulders, rather dark-complexioned, with a very pleasant countenance, and coming closer, his eyes caught with mine.

Seeing how fearful I was, he began to speak. "Fear not. I am sent from the presence of Almighty God to tell you that your peculiar life and your misunderstood ways have been to indicate that God has sent you to take a gift of divine healing to the people of the world. If you will be sincere, and can get the people to believe you, nothing shall stand before your prayer, not even cancer."

The "angel" also said that Branham would detect diseases by "vibrations on his left hand."[39]

Branham began his ministry as an independent evangelist. During "revival" tent meetings in Jeffersonville, Indiana, in 1933, he preached to three thousand each evening. He baptized 130 believers at the concluding service. His friend Pearry Green said that "a heavenly light appeared above him as he was about to baptize the seventeenth person."[40] After the crusade, his followers built Branham Tabernacle in Jeffersonville. Other independent Baptist ministers in the area avoided him because of his mystical teaching.

During these Depression years, Branham attended a "Jesus only" Pentecostal meeting. The people welcomed him and invited him to preach. He later preached in several other Pentecostal churches.

During a Sunday evening service in his own church on May 7, 1946, he received a telegram from a pastor friend, Robert Daugherty, who asked him to come to St. Louis to pray for his sick daughter.

Branham did, and the girl recovered.

Daugherty was so impressed that he asked the evangelist to conduct revival services in his church. From June 14 to June 25, 1946, Branham held a healing campaign.

Then he held another in Jonesboro, Arkansas, where he reportedly raised a man from the dead. Some twenty-five thousand from twenty-eight states and Mexico crowded the meetings. At Camden, when Branham's picture was taken, "a supernatural light appeared above his head."

The evangelist was conducted from town to town, mostly in "Oneness Pentecostal" circles, "bringing salvation and healing to throngs of anxious seekers who dared to believe his story of angelic visitation and endowment of the healing power of Jesus Christ," as one admirer wrote.[41]

In 1947, Branham acquired Gordon Lindsay as his manager. Lindsay, later founder of Christ for the Nations school, edited the *Voice of Healing* magazine, which advertized the multiple healing evangelists of the day.

At that time, Branham was popular among most Pentecostals and leaders, such as Oral Roberts, A. A. Allen, and George Warnock. Demos Shakarian and his Full Gospel Business Men's Fellowship acclaimed Branham's ministry. The editor of *Voice*, the FGBMFI's magazine, wrote in 1961, "In Bible Days, there were men of God who were Prophets and Seers. But in all the Sacred Records, none of these had a greater ministry than that of William Branham."[42]

This popularity continued until the 1960s, when the evangelist became controversial because of the aberrant doctrines he developed. Although denying he had embraced "oneness" theology, for instance, he insisted that Christians baptized in the trinitarian tradition be rebaptized in the name of Jesus only. He also taught that God was one person with three different "attributes": the Father, Son, and Holy Spirit. The doctrine of the Trinity, he said, was the "Babylonian" foundation of "the denominations."[43]

Moreover, Branham had an aberrant view of the Bible. He believed that God gave his Word in three forms: the Zodiac, the Egyptian pyramids, and the written Scriptures.[44]

Most controversial was Branham's "serpent's seed" doctrine. Satan, he said, in the guise of the serpent, seduced Eve in the Garden of Eden and had sexual relations with her. She produced Cain, the "serpent's seed," and his descendants are bound for hell. Those who accepted Branham's teaching were the "seed of God" and would become the Bride of Christ. Although he considered denominationalism "the mark of the Beast," he acknowledged that some would be saved in denominational churches. However, they would have to go through the Great Tribulation.

Proclaiming himself as the angel of Revelation 3:14 and 10:7, Branham predicted that the World Council of Churches, under the control of Roman Catholicism, would dissolve all denominations by 1977. Then Christ would come for his Bride and destroy the world.

Critics not only cited his doctrines as suspect, but his visions and healing methods as well. Throughout his lifetime, Branham depended on his "angel" for guidance. Just before a healing service in Germany, he told his interpreter, an American-German minister, "Don't stand to the right of me because my angel stands there."

"What does your angel look like?" the interpreter asked.

Branham described a "well-built man with dark hair" who stood with folded arms. "I can only do what my angel tells me to do," he explained. "He's with me day and night, and if I don't do what he says, I have no authority in my preaching. I can't even decide things in my own private life and can only go out or see people if the angel allows me to."

Branham often fell into a trance while preaching. Afterwards, he would be completely exhausted.

Once the interpreter asked him, "Do you think your power to heal people comes from the Holy Spirit?"

"No, my angel does it."

At this, the interpreter quit working for him.[45]

Branham once met a man actively involved in the occult. Unaware of who he was, the evangelist said, "You look exactly like the angel which appears to me every day."[46]

Although Branham died on Christmas Eve in 1965 in a head-on collision with a drunk driver, many followers believed he would rise from the dead in three days. Some claimed he was virgin-born and was God incarnate.[47]

The influence of Branham's "divinely inspired" prophecies and teaching continues today. No doubt learned from Kenyon's writings, he emphasized the power of the spoken word.

This emphasis is now proclaimed by faith-movement teachers. Many consider Branham a prophet.

## The Latter-Rain Movement

Since the turn of the century, Pentecostals have used the term *Latter Rain* to refer to the Pentecostal movement itself or to an outpouring of the Holy Spirit in the "end times" before Christ's return. This outpouring would be accompanied by signs and wonders.

More generally, the term *Latter Rain* is used for a specific Pentecostal movement in the late 1940s. Characterized by reported healings and miracles, it was thought to be the fulfillment of Joel 2:23—the outpouring of the Holy Spirit before the imminent, premillenial return of Christ.

The movement began in Sharon Orphanage and Schools in North Battleford, Saskatchewan, Canada, under the direction of Herrick Holt and George and Ern Hawtin.

In the fall of 1947, healing evangelist William Branham held a campaign in Vancouver, British Columbia, Canada. Several teachers from the Sharon schools attended the meetings. Impressed by Branham's miraculous knowledge of illness and healing powers, they accepted his doctrines.

Back at the school, these teachers encouraged their students to gather for Bible study, prayer, and fasting. Supernatural signs and healings followed.

Because of a long dearth of such manifestations in classical Pentecostalism, people flocked to see the miracles taking place at North Battleford. They came from many parts of North America and the world. In turn, they invited Sharon teachers to minister in their home areas. The movement quickly spread through the Assemblies of God in both Canada and the United States.

By 1949, Latter Rain's momentum moved from North Battleford to other centers, notably Elim Bible Institute in New York State; Bethesda Missionary Temple in Detroit, Michigan; and the Apostolic Church denomination.

That same year, the general council of the Assemblies of God denounced the "New Order of the Latter Rain," as it came to be known, because of its aberrant doctrines and practices. The problem was that its leaders had developed their teachings from Franklin Hall and William Branham. As has been noted earlier, these men combined Pentecostalism with occultism.

Through the Latter-Rain "revivals," the heretical teachings of Hall and Branham spread quickly through the whole Pentecostal system. Those independent ministries who accepted this teaching gradually weeded out the more peculiar doctrines, but Latter-Rain theology was "developed directly from combining the distinctive emphases of Hall and Branham."[48]

Theologian Robert Bowman, formerly of the Christian Research Institute, points to these elements in Latter-Rain theology:

1. *Restorationism.* God has been restoring "new truth" to his church since the Reformation, including Latter-Rain teachings.

2. *Immortalization.* Believers will overcome death and attain immortality before Christ's return.

3. *Healing.* Believers should expect divine healing, not merely request it.

4. *Faith.* By the force of faith, believers can "create new realities out of nothing, just as God created the world out of nothing."

5. *Fivefold ministry.* The church today receives new revelation and direction through all five offices of Ephesians 4:11, including apostles and prophets. "Church unity comes through submission to the elders and through them to the fivefold ministry."[49]

The Latter Rain also emphasized "distinctive spiritual disciplines": 1) deliverance of believers from demons; 2) extended fasting "to attain supernatural power over the body"; 3) laying on of hands, especially for healing; 4) unrestrained and extended periods of praise in services,[50] often to the neglect of solid Bible instruction.

Brooks of Latter-Rain teachings and practices flowed into the charismatic-renewal stream of the 1960s and 1970s. This resulted in such mixtures as the Manifest Sons of God, the shepherding movement, and the faith movement.

How should mainstream, evangelical churches respond to aberrant groups today? Theologian Michael Horton suggests:

"Under the supposed banner of unity, we have harbored enemy ships—as long as they flew our flag. That policy must change. Tolerating enemies of the historic Christian faith as though they were our brethren is not love, but adultery. The substance of the faith is the only basis for unity."[51]

# Endnotes

Chapter 3 *Going with the Flow*

1. Flo Conway and Jim Siegelman, "Information Disease," *Science Digest* (January 1982): 92.
2. Robert M. Bowman Jr. with Craig S. Hawkins and Dan R. Schlesinger, "The Gospel According to Paul: A Critique of 'Kingdom Theology,'" *Christian Research Journal* (Winter/Spring 1988): 10.
3. Shirl Short, "The Menace of the New Cults," *Moody Monthly* (July-August 1977): 27.
4. Walter Martin, *The New Cults* (Santa Ana, Calif.: Vision House, 1980), 143.
5. Martin, *The New Cults*, 196–197.
6. Ibid.
7. Ibid., 37–39.
8. Ibid.
9. Richard Abanes, "The Branch Davidians," Statement No. DD-025 (San Juan Capistrano, Calif.: Christian Research Institute, 1993), 4.
10. Conway and Siegelman, "Information Disease," 92.

Chapter 4 *Charisma and Pride*

1. Albert Speer, *Spandau: The Secret Diaries* (New York: MacMillan, 1976), 81.
2. William L. Shirer, *The Nightmare Years* (Boston: Little, Brown, 1984), 127.
3. Shirer, *The Nightmare Years*, 127.
4. Ibid., 128.
5. Ibid., 131.
6. Ronald M. Enroth, *Youth, Brainwashing, and the Extremist Cults* (Grand Rapids: Zondervan, 1977), 108–109.

7. S. T. Coleridge, *The Devil's Thoughts*, as quoted in John Bartlett, ed., *Bartlett's Familiar Quotations* (Boston: Little, Brown, 1882, 1980), 435:17.
8. Diane Sawyer, "Men of God," ABC *PrimeTime Live*, 21 November 1992.
9. Abanes, "The Branch Davidians," 4.
10. Walter B. Knight, ed., *Knight's Master Book of New Illustrations* (Grand Rapids: Eerdmans, 1956), 312.

## Chapter 5 *Anger and Intimidation*

1. General Hans Guderian, *Panzer Leader* (New York, 1952), 343, as quoted in William L. Shirer, *A Native's Return* (New York: Simon and Schuster, 1976), 12.
2. Abanes, "The Branch Davidians," 2–6.
3. Nathan H. Harriman, "Inside Story of Sanfordism and Shiloh," *Lewiston Evening Journal*, 26 September 1903, 1–3, 10.
4. Frank S. Murray, *The Sublimity of Faith* (Amherst, N. H.: The Kingdom Press, 1981), 208–209.
5. Herbert Lockyer, *The Sins of Saints* (London: Pickering & Inglis, n.d.), 14.
6. Craig Massey, "Anger: The Destroyer Within," *Moody Monthly* (January 1985): 79.
7. John A. MacMillan, *The Authority of the Believer* (Harrisburg, Penn.: Christian Publications, 1980), 50.
8. Ibid., 84.

## Chapter 6 *Greed and Fraud*

1. Russell Watson, et al., "Heaven Can Wait," *Newsweek* (8 June 1987): 62, 69.
2. "Two Brothers Receive Stiff Prison Sentences on Tax Charges," *The Seattle Times*, 9 September 1989, A11.
3. Ibid.
4. "Jim Bakker Sentenced to 45 Years," *The Seattle Times*, 24 October 1989, A1.
5. "News," *Christianity Today* (28 October 1991): 39.
6. "Convicted Ex-Televangelist Is Released to Halfway House," *The Seattle Times*, 1 July 1994, A5.
7. Ken Garfield, "Bakker Back, Preaching to the Faithful," *The Seattle Times*, 13 February 1995, A6.
8. Jamie Buckingham, "Philistines and the Media," *Charisma* (January 1992): 90.
9. Les and Joanne Coughran, "Bethesda Christian Center: Where Creative Gifts Are Encouraged," *Christian Life* (January 1980): 31–33.
10. Laura Parker, "'Pastor Was God,' Says Church Theft Defendant," *Seattle Post-Intelligencer*, 26 March 1980, A1.
11. "Ex-Church Official Blames Minister," *The Seattle Times*, 25 March 1980, Al.

12. Parker, "'Pastor Was God,'" A1.
13. "Church's Ex-Manager: Pastor 'Mesmerized' Him," *The Seattle Times*, 26 March 1980.
14. "Wenatchee Religion," *The Everett Herald*, 29 May 1980, B11.
15. Sawyer, "Men of God," TV program.
16. Ibid.
17. Edward E. Plowman, "Jonestown Question Marks Abound One Year After Tragedy," *Christianity Today* (16 November 1979): 42–45.
18. Bonnie Thielmann with Dean Merrill, *The Broken God* (Elgin, Ill.: David C. Cook, 1979), 75–77.
19. Robert Tilton, ministry letter (Dallas: Robert Tilton Ministries, n.d.), 2–5.
20. Howard Swindle, "Televangelist Sued Over Letters to Dead Man," *The Seattle Times*, 28 February 1992, A2.
21. Karen M. Thomas, "Probes Target Evangelist," *The Seattle Times*, 30 March 1992, A8.
22. Tilton, ministry letter.
23. Ibid.
24. Paul Carden, "Special Report: Tilton's Tottering TV Empire," *Christian Research Journal* (Summer 1992): 5.
25. Thielmann, *Broken God*, 51, 74–76.
26. Sawyer, "Men of God," TV program.
27. Ibid.
28. Mark Harden, "Little of Donations Went to Orphans, Witnesses Say," *The Everett Herald*, 13 August 1981, A3.
29. Harden, "Little of Donations," A3.
30. Ibid.
31. Thielmann, *Broken God*, 72.
32. Tilton, ministry letter.
33. Personal interview with authors. Name and notes on file.
34. Sawyer, "Men of God," TV program.
35. Ibid.
36. Randy Frame, "Did Oral Roberts Go Too Far?" *Christianity Today* (20 February 1987): 43.
37. Frame, "Oral Roberts," 44.
38. Ibid.
39. Joe Mooney, "A Prophet's Vision: Religion Geared to Ordinary People," *Seattle Post-Intelligencer*, 5 July 1987.
40. Frame, "Oral Roberts," 45.
41. Mooney, "A Prophet's Vision," *Seattle Post-Intelligencer*.
42. Perucci Ferraiuolo and Paul Carden, "Where Are They Now? A Televangelist Update," *Christian Research Journal* (Fall 1994): 7.
43. Ferraiuolo and Carden, "Where Are They Now?" 8.
44. Ibid., 45.
45. Arthur T. Pierson, *George Muller of Bristol* (London: Pickering & Inglis, 1899), 70.

Chapter 7 *Immorality*

1. Charles R. Swindoll, *Moral Purity* (Fullerton, Calif.: Insight for Living, 1985), 22.
2. Larry Martz, et al., "God and Money," *Newsweek* (6 April 1987): 16–17.
3. Martz, "God and Money," 18–19.
4. Ibid., 17.
5. Ibid.
6. "Self-Described Prostitute in Swaggart Car," *The Seattle Times*, 12 October 1991, A7.
7. "Swaggart: God Says, 'It's None of Your Business,'" *The Seattle Times*, 17 October 1991, A5.
8. "Swaggart's TV Ministry to Dwindle, Maybe End," *The Seattle Times*, 27 October 1991, A12.
9. Ferraiuolo and Carden, "Where Are They Now?" 8.
10. John Hessburg, "Vashon Pastor Denies Sex Accusations," *The Seattle Times*, 15 May 1983, A1.
11. Hessburg, "Vashon Pastor," A1.
12. Ibid., A3.
13. Ibid., A1.
14. Ibid.
15. Ibid.
16. Ibid., A3.
17. John McCoy, "The Fear of Demons, the Death of a Child," *Seattle Post-Intelligencer*, 10 April 1986, A1.
18. Ibid.
19. Ibid., A8.
20. Ibid., A1.
21. Marsha King, "Burien Pastor Dismissed by Church Elders," *The Seattle Times*, 5 March 1988, A1.
22. Mary Rothschild, "Adultery Not Over, Ex-Sect Member Says," *Seattle Post-Intelligencer*, 11 March 1988, A1, 8.
23. Marsha King, "Church Gathers in Separate Camps," *The Seattle Times*, 12 March 1988, A1.
24. Personal interview with authors. Names and notes on file.
25. McCoy, "The Fear of Demons," A8.
26. Jim Haley, "Ted Rinaldo Emerges to Find His Eden Undone," *The Everett Herald*, 17 August 1987, A1, 8.
27. Personal interview with authors. Names and notes on file.
28. Paul Carden, Richard Abanes, and Ken Samples, "The Branch Davidians: An Interview with David Bunds," *The Bible Answer Man*, heard on KGNW, Seattle, Wash., March 1993.
29. Abanes, "The Branch Davidians," 3.
30. Harrison Rainie, et al., "The Final Days of David Koresh," *U. S. News and World Report* (3 May 1993): 30.
31. "Waco Cult Children Tell of Sex, Paddlings," *The Seattle Times*, 4 May 1993, A5.

32. Personal interview with authors. Names and notes on file.
33. "A Talk with MacDonalds," *Christianity Today* (10 July 1987): 38.

Chapter 8 *Enslaving Authoritarian Structure*
  1. William B. Breuer, *Retaking the Philippines* (New York: St. Martin's Press, 1986), 103–105.
  2. Herman Wouk, *The Caine Mutiny* (Garden City, N.Y.: Doubleday, 1951), 334.
  3. Carden, et al., "Branch Davidians: Interview."
  4. Robert Lindsey, "Many Sect Leaders Take Control of Members' Lives," *The Daily Breeze*, 5 July 1986, D2.
  5. Ron and Vicki Burks, *Damaged Disciples: Casualties of Authoritarian Churches and the Shepherding Movement* (Grand Rapids: Zondervan, 1992), 95.
  6. Burks, *Damaged Disciples*, 96–97.
  7. Ibid., 90–91.
  8. Don Lattin, "The Shepherding Movement," *San Francisco Sunday Examiner and Chronicle*, 19 February 1984, A4.
  9. Burks, *Damaged Disciples*, 58.
 10. Ibid., 90.
 11. Ibid., 91.
 12. Randy Frame, "A Team of Cult Watchers Challenges a Growing Campus Ministry," *Christianity Today* (10 August 1984): 40.
 13. Personal interview with authors. Names and notes on file.
 14. Frame, "Team of Cult Watchers," 38.
 15. Ibid., 43.
 16. Lattin, "Shepherding Movement," A4.
 17. Ibid., A1.
 18. Ibid., A5.
 19. Ibid., A4.
 20. Ibid.
 21. As quoted by James Hamann, "Authority and Submission," typescript of sermon, n.d.
 22. Burks, *Damaged Disciples*, 58.
 23. Derek Prince, *Discipleship, Shepherding, Commitment* (Ft. Lauderdale, Fla.: Derek Prince Publications, 1976), 19.
 24. Ibid., 19.
 25. Ibid., 19–20.
 26. Bill Counts, "The Evangelical Orthodox Church and the New Covenant Apostolic Order," (Berkeley, Calif.: Spiritual Counterfeits Project, 1979), 2.
 27. Bob Mumford, *The Problem of Doing Your Own Thing* (Ft. Lauderdale, Fla.: Bob Mumford, 1973), 39.
 28. Mumford, *The Problem*, 68.
 29. Personal interview with authors. Names and notes on file.
 30. Personal interview with authors. Names and notes on file.

31. Prince, *Discipleship,* 18.
32. Counts, "The Evangelical Orthodox Church," 5.
33. Burks, *Damaged Disciples,* 139.
34. Jan Karel Van Baalen, *The Chaos of Cults: A Study in Present-Day Isms* (Grand Rapids: Eerdmans, 1962), 364.
35. W. E. Vine, *An Expository Dictionary of New Testament Words* (London: Oliphants, 1953), 124.
36. L. E. Maxwell, "Perspective," *The Prairie Overcomer* (January 1957): 31.
37. Abraham Lincoln, speech at Edwardsville, Ill., 11 September 1858, as quoted in John Bartlett, ed., *Bartlett's Familiar Quotations* (Boston: Little, Brown, 1980), 520.

## Chapter 9 *Exclusivity*

1. Melinda Liu and Todd Barrett, "Hard Lessons in the Ashes," *Newsweek* (3 May 1993): 31.
2. Carden, et al., "Branch Dividians: Interview."
3. Ibid.
4. Linda Medill Hall, personal interview with authors. Notes on file.
5. Walter Martin, *The Kingdom of the Cults* (Minneapolis: Bethany House, 1985), 26–29.
6. Ronald M. Enroth, "Churches on the Fringe," *Eternity* (October 1986): 17.
7. Personal interview with authors. Names and notes on file.
8. Counts, "The Evangelical Orthodox Church," 5.
9. Ray Ruppert, "From Unrest to Rebellion," *The Seattle Times,* 13 June 1981, A1, 11.
10. Ray Ruppert, "Dissidents Say Church Uses Fear," *The Seattle Times,* 12 June 1981, A1, 10.
11. Ray Ruppert, "Couple Feels the Sting of Force Detachment," *The Seattle Times,* 18 March 1988, A1, 9.
12. Marsha King, "Barnett's Troubles Obscure His Gifts," *The Seattle Times,* 18 March 1988, A1, 9.
13. Enroth, "Churches on the Fringe," 19.
14. Personal interview with authors. Names and notes on file.
15. Counts, "The Evangelical Orthodox Church," 4.

## Chapter 10 *Demanding Loyalty and Honor*

1. Fred Bayles and Robert Dvorchak, "Diverse Group Followed Koresh to Their Deaths," *The Seattle Times,* 25 April 1993, A7.
2. Barbara Kantrowitz, et al., "Day of Judgment," *Newsweek* (3 May 1993): 27.
3. Personal interview with authors. Names and notes on file.
4. Ibid.
5. Ibid.
6. Ibid.

7. Personal interview with authors. Names and notes on file.
8. Counts, "The Evangelical Orthodox Church," 3.
9. Ibid., 4.
10. Watson, et at., "Heaven Can Wait," 59.
11. Richard N. Ostling, "TV's Unholy War," *Time* (6 April 1987): 67.
12. Richard N. Ostling, "At Home with Jim," *Time* (8 June 1987): 72.
13. Dave Breese, "When to Bail Out," *Christian Life* (April 1979): 35.
14. Ronald M. Enroth, "The Power Abusers," *Eternity* (October 1979): 35.
15. Daniel Stewart, "Loyalty Among Christians," *A Lamp Unto My Feet* (December 1978): 1.
16. "Of Shepherds, Fiefs, and the Flocks," *Christianity Today* (10 October 1980): 14.
17. Dave Breese, *Know the Marks of Cults* (Wheaton, Ill.: Victor, 1979), 102.
18. Stewart, "Loyalty Among Christians," 1.
19. "Of Shepherds," *Christianity Today*, 14.
20. Roland H. Bainton, *The Church of Our Fathers* (Philadelphia: Westminster Press, 1941), 135.

Chapter 11 *"New" Extrabiblical Revelation*

1. Breese, *Know the Marks of Cults*, 25.
2. Walter Lord, *A Night to Remember* (New York: Bantam Books, 1956), 1–2.
3. Don Lynch, *Titanic: An Illustrated History* (New York: Hyperion, 1992), 93.
4. Lord, *A Night to Remember*, 80.
5. Jeremy C. Jackson, *No Other Foundation* (Westchester, Ill.: Cornerstone Books, 1980), 38.
6. Breese, *Know the Marks of Cults*, 25–26.
7. Stanley M. Burgess and Gary B. McGee, eds., *Dictionary of Pentecostal and Charismatic Movements* (Grand Rapids: Zondervan, 1988), 719.
8. D. R. McConnell, *A Different Gospel* (Peabody, Mass.: Hendrickson Publishers, 1988), 186.
9. Ibid., 187.
10. William M. Alnor and Robert Lyle, "Controversial Prophetic Movement Is Incorporated into the Vineyard," *Christian Research Journal* (Fall 1990): 5.
11. Dennis and Rita Bennett, *The Holy Spirit and You* (Plainfield, N.J.: Logos, 1971), 99.
12. Ibid., 99.
13. Ibid., 110.
14. A prophecy given in a small-group meeting. In authors' file.
15. Merrill F. Unger, *The Baptism and Gifts of the Holy Spirit* (Chicago: Moody Press, 1974), 140.
16. Ibid., 141.

17. Ibid., 141.
18. Neil Babcox, *A Search for Charismatic Reality* (Portland, Ore.: Multnomah Press, 1985), 52–53.
19. Ibid., 53–54.
20. Ibid., 57.
21. Counts, "The Evangelical Orthodox Church," 2.
22. Dick Ballew, *The Place Where God Lives* (Mt. Hermon.: Calif.: Conciliar Press, n.d), 8, as quoted by Counts, "The Evangelical Orothdox Church."
23. Pete Gillquist, *Fresh New Insight into Love Is Now*, 122, as quoted by Counts, "The Evangelical Orthodox Church," 2.
24. Counts, "The Evangelical Orthodox Church," 2.
25. Ostling, "TV's Unholy War," 63.
26. Kenneth E. Hagin, *I Believe in Visions* (Tulsa, Okla.: Faith Library Publications, 1984), 97–124.
27. Robert Tilton, "March 17th Is Your Miracle Day!" (Dallas, Texas: Robert Tilton Ministries, n.d.), 3.
28. Ibid., 6.
29. Ferraiuolo and Carden, "Where Are They Now?" 45.
30. Joe Maxwell, "Is Laughing for the Lord Holy?" *Christianity Today* (24 October 1994): 78–79.
31. Randy Frame, "Critics Claim 'Word-Faith' Is Cultic," *Christianity Today* (24 October 1994): 85.
32. Jackson, *No Other Foundation*, 34.
33. As quoted by Mike Atkinson, "New Cult Targets Christians," *Logos* (March/April 1978).
34. "An Interview with Juan Carlos Ortiz," *Logos* (January/February 1980): 34–41.

Chapter 12 *How to Get Out of the Whirlpool*
1. "Shiloh—A Tragedy and Not a Joke," *Lewiston Saturday Journal*, 27 October 1906, 1.

Chapter 13 *How to Get Back Into the Mainstream*
1. Harriman, "Inside Story of Sanfordism and Shiloh," 10–11.
2. Ibid.
3. Ibid.
4. Ibid., 11.
5. "Doctors Called in Sandford Case," *Lewiston Evening Journal*, 6 October 1905, 10.
6. Personal interview with authors. Names and notes on file.
7. Breese, *Know the Marks of Cults*, 48–49.
8. "Of Shepherds, Fiefs and the Flocks," *Christianity Today*, 14.

Chapter 14 *A Community of the Holy*
1. Frank Sandford, *Tongues of Fire*, January 1897, 16.

2. "Grandfather Dunlap Gets Boy," *Lewiston Saturday Journal*, 13 May 1905, 14.
3. Murray, *The Sublimity of Faith*, 24, 34.
4. Arnold L. White, *The Almighty and Us* (Ft. Lauderdale, Fla.: n.p., 1979), 41.
5. Murray, *The Sublimity of Faith*, 296.
6. White, *The Almighty and Us*, 82.
7. "Manslaughter Charge Now," *Lewiston Evening Journal*, 4 February 1904, 1–3.
8. White, *The Almighty and Us*, 83.
9. Murray, *The Sublimity of Faith*, 214.
10. Estella Sheller, "A Tacoma Woman Tells of Life in Shiloh," *Lewiston Evening Journal*, 21 October 1904, 9.
11. Sheller, "A Tacoma Woman," 9.
12. Harriman, "Inside Story of Sanfordism and Shiloh," 11.
13. Murray, *The Sublimity of Faith*, 129.
14. Harriman, "Inside Story of Sanfordism and Shiloh," 10.
15. Ibid.
16. "Miss Harriman Dead," *Lewiston Evening Journal*, 16 August 1906, 3.
17. "Shiloh Leaders Refused to Let Her See Sick Son," *Lewiston Evening Journal*, 26 October 1911, 11.
18. White, *The Almighty and Us*, 102.
19. "Another Impression," *Lewiston Evening Journal*, 18 December 1911, 12.
20. "A Restraining Hand Is Needed," *Lewiston Evening Journal*, 23 October 1911, 8.
21. "Shiloh Leaders Refused," *Lewiston Evening Journal*, 1, 11.
22. "Habeas Corpus Writ Issed," *Lewiston Evening Journal*, 6 June 1910, 1.
23. Murray, *The Sublimity of Faith*, 481.
24. "Sandford 'Guilty,' Says the Jury," *Lewiston Evening Journal*, 9 December 1911, 1, 9.
25. "Sandford Held in $10,000 Bonds," *Lewiston Evening Journal*, 2 November 1911, 8.
26. "Sandford Held," *Lewiston Evening Journal*, 8.
27. White, *The Almighty and Us*, 271–272.
28. "Sandford Again Under Arrest," *Lewiston Evening Journal*, 25 October 1911, 1.
29. "Sandford Released," *Lewiston Evening Journal*, 28 October 1911, 12.
30. "Rev. Frank W. Sandford Indicted at Portland on Six Different Counts," *Lewiston Evening Journal*, 8 December 1911, 1.
31. "Sandford 'Guilty,'" *Lewiston Evening Journal*, 1, 9.
32. "Another Impression," *Lewiston Evening Journal*, 12.
33. "Rev. Frank W. Sandford Given Ten Years at the Federal Prison, Atlanta," *Lewiston Evening Journal*, 18 December 1911, 1.
34. "Sandford Leaves for Atlanta," *Lewiston Evening Journal*, 19 December 1911, 6.
35. Murray, *The Sublimity of Faith*, 574.

36. Ibid., 584.
37. Ibid., 601–603.
38. Ibid., 331.

Appendix

1. Salem Kirban, *Christian Science* (Chicago: Moody Press, 1974), 3–4.
2. Van Baalen, *Chaos of Cults*, 130.
3. Ralph Waldo Trine, *In Tune With the Infinite* (New York: Bobbs-Merrill, 1970), 15–16.
4. Ralph Waldo Trine, *The Winning of the Best* (Indianapolis: Bobbs-Merrill, n.d.), 64.
5. As quoted by Robert T. Handy, *A History of the Churches in the United States and Canada* (New York: Oxford University Press, 1977), 338.
6. Trine, *In Tune*, 141.
7. McConnell, *A Different Gospel*, 174.
8. Van Baalen, *Chaos of Cults*, 87.
9. Kirban, *Christian Science*, 17.
10. Van Baalen, *Chaos of Cults*, 87–88.
11. Kirban, *Christian Science*, 33–40.
12. Josh McDowell and Don Stewart, *Handbook of Today's Religions* (San Bernardino, Calif.: Here's Life Publishers, 1983), 123.
13. Mary Baker Eddy, *Science and Health with Key to the Scriptures* (Boston: Trustees, 1934), 590, as quoted in McConnell, *A Different Gospel*, 106.
14. Eddy, *Science and Health*, 330.
15. "Man Is, Not Shall Be, Perfect and Immortal," *Christian Science Sentinel*, 22 December 1934, 327, as quoted in John R. Rice, *False Doctrines Answered from the Scriptures* (Murfreesboro, Tenn.: Sword of the Lord Publishers, 1970), 132.
16. Eddy, *Science and Health*, 428.
17. Ibid., 495.
18. Ibid., 390.
19. McDowell and Stewart, *Handbook*, 124–130.
20. Ibid., 131–132.
21. *Unity*, Vol. 57, no. 5, 464, as quoted by McDowell and Stewart, *Handbook*, 133.
22. *Ibid.*, 134.
23. Charles Fillmore, *Christian Healing* (Unity Village, Mo.: Unity, n.d.), 16.
24. H. E. Cady, *How I Used Truth* (Lee's Summit, Mo.: Unity, n.d.), 64.
25. *Unity*, as quoted by McDowell and Stewart, *Handbook*, 135.
26. Burgess and McGee, *Dictionary*, 517.
27. Marc Galanter, *Cults: Faith, Healing, and Coercion* (New York: Oxford University Press, 1989), 38.
28. David Edwin Harrell, Jr., *All Things Are Possible: The Healing and Charismatic Revivals in Modern America* (Bloomington, Ind.: Indiana University Press, 1975), 80–81.

29. Albert James Dager, *Vengeance Is Ours* (Redmond, Wash.: Sword Publishers, 1990), 50.
30. Harrell, *All Things Are Possible*, 81.
31. Franklin Hall, "Will You Be Crucified in 1962?" *Miracle Magazine* (May 1962): 12–14, as quoted in Harrell, *All Things Are Possible*, 212.
32. "An Open Safety Pin Was Removed From My Stomach!" *Miracle Magazine* (January 1960): 4–5, as quoted in Harrell, *All Things Are Possible*, 213.
33. "I Took My Cancer to Church in a Jar," *Miracle Magazine* (January 1960): 7, as quoted in Dager, *Vengeance Is Ours*, 51.
34. "I Lost Over 200 Pounds When I Used God's Reducing Plan," *Miracle Magazine* (January 1961): 3, as quoted in Harrell, *All Things Are Possible*, 213.
35. Dager, *Vengeance Is Ours*, 52.
36. Ibid.
37. Burgess and McGee, *Dictionary*, 95.
38. William M. Branham, *My Life Story* (Jefferson, Ind.: Spoken Word Publications, n.d.), 19.
39. Gordon Lindsay, *William Branham: A Man Sent from God* (Jeffersonville, Ind.: William Branham, 1950), as quoted in Harrell, *All Things Are Possible*, 28.
40. Lindsay, *William Branham*, 43, 71.
41. Harrell, *All Things Are Possible*, 30.
42. Ibid., 162.
43. Dager, *Vengeance Is Ours*, 55.
44. Ibid.
45. Kurt Koch, *Occult Bondage and Deliverance* (Grand Rapids: Kregel Publications, 1971), 48–50.
46. Ibid., 51.
47. Dager, *Vengeance Is Ours*, 59.
48. Bowman, et al., "The Gospel According to Paulk," 12.
49. Ibid., 12–13.
50. Ibid.
51. Michael Horton, ed., *The Agony of Deceit: What Some TV Preachers Are Really Teaching* (Chicago: Moody Press, 1990), 22.

# Bibliography

Appel, Willa. *Cults in America.* New York: Henry Holt & Co., 1983.

Babcox, Neil. *A Search for Charismatic Reality.* Portland, Ore.: Multnomah Press, 1985.

Bainton, Roland H. *The Church of Our Fathers.* Philadelphia: Westminster Press, 1941.

Ballew, Dick. *The Place Where God Lives.* Mt. Hermon, Calif.: Conciliar Press, n.d.

Bennett, Dennis and Rita. *The Holy Spirit and You.* Plainfield, N.J.: Logos, 1971.

Boa, Kenneth. *Cults, World Religions and You.* Wheaton, Ill.: Victor Books, 1977.

Bowman, Robert M., Jr. with Craig S. Hawkins and Dan R. Schlesinger. "The Gospel According to Paulk: A Critique of 'Kingdom Theology.'" *Christian Research Journal* (Winter/Spring 1988).

Branham, William M. *My Life Story.* Jefferson, Ind.: Spoken Word Publications, n.d.

Breese, Dave. *Know the Marks of Cults.* Wheaton, Ill.: Victor Books, 1979.

Breuer, William B. *Retaking the Philippines.* New York: St. Martin's Press, 1986.

Burgess, Stanley M. and Gary B. McGee, eds. *Dictionary of*

*Pentecostal and Charismatic Movements.* Grand Rapids: Zondervan, 1988.

Burks, Ron and Vicki. *Damaged Disciples: Casualties of Authoritarian Churches and the Shepherding Movement.* Grand Rapids: Zondervan, 1992.

Cady, H. E. *How I Used Truth.* Lee's Summit, Mo.: Unity, n.d.

Cohen, Daniel. *The New Believers: Young Religion in America.* New York: Ballantine Books, 1975.

Conway, Flo and Jim Siegelman. *Snapping: America's Epidemic of Sudden Personality Change.* New York: J. B. Lippincott, 1978.

Dager, Albert James. *Vengeance Is Ours.* Redmond, Wash.: Sword Publishers, 1990.

Eddy, Mary Baker. *Science and Health with Key to the Scriptures.* Boston: Trustees, 1934.

Edwards, Christopher. *Crazy for God: The Nightmare of Cult Life.* Englewood Cliffs, N.J.: Prentice-Hall, 1979.

Ehrenborg, Todd. "The Church of the Living Word" in *The New Cults.* Walter Martin, ed. Santa Ana: Vision House, 1980, 269–296.

Eisenberg, Gary D. *Smashing the Idols: A Jewish Inquiry into the Cult Phenomenon.* Northvale, N.J.: Jason Aronson, Inc., 1988.

Enroth, Ronald M. *Churches That Abuse.* Grand Rapids: Zondervan, 1992.

———. *The Lure of the Cults.* Chappaquah, N.Y.: Christian Herald Books, 1979.

———. *Youth, Brainwashing, and the Extremist Cults.* Grand Rapids: Zondervan, 1977.

Fillmore, Charles. *Christian Healing.* Unity Village, Mo.: Unity, n.d.

Galanter, Marc. *Cults: Faith, Healing, and Coercion.* New York: Oxford University Press, 1989.

Greenleaf, Robert K. *Servant Leadership: A Journey into the*

*Nature of Legitimate Power and Greatness.* New York: Paulist Press, 1977.

Hagin, Kenneth E. *I Believe in Visions.* Tulsa, Okla.: Faith Library Publications, 1984.

Hagin, Kenneth E. *The Name of Jesus.* Tulsa, Okla.: Kenneth Hagin Ministries, 1979.

Handy, Robert T. *A History of the Churches in the United States and Canada.* New York: Oxford University Press, 1977.

Hanegraaff, Hank. *Christianity in Crisis.* Eugene, Ore.: Harvest House, 1993.

Harrell, David Edwin, Jr. *All Things Are Possible: The Healing and Charismatic Revivals in Modern America.* Bloomington, Ind.: Indiana University Press, 1975.

Horton, Michael, ed. *The Agony of Deceit: What Some TV Preachers Are Really Teaching.* Chicago: Moody Press, 1990.

Irvine, William C. *Heresies Exposed.* New York: Loizeaux Brothers, 1917, 1945.

Jackson, Jeremy C. *No Other Foundation.* Westchester, Ill.: Cornerstone Books, 1980.

Kantrowitz, Barbara, et al. "Day of Judgment." *Newsweek* (3 May 1993): 27.

Kenyon, E. W. *Jesus the Healer.* Kenyon Gospel Publishing Society, 1968.

Kirban, Salem. *Christian Science.* Chicago: Moody Press, 1974.

Knight, Walter B., ed. *Knight's Master Book of New Illustrations.* Grand Rapids: Eerdmans, 1956.

Koch, Kurt. *Occult Bondage and Deliverance.* Grand Rapids: Kregel Publications, 1971.

LeBar, James J. *Cults, Sects, and the New Age.* Huntington, Ind.: Our Sunday Visitor, Inc., 1989.

Lifton, Robert J. *Thought Reform and the Psychology of Totalism.* New York: W. W. Norton and Co., 1961.

Lindsay, Gordon. *William Branham: A Man Sent from God.* Jeffersonville, Ind.: William Branham, 1950.

Lockyer, Herbert. *The Sins of the Saints.* London: Pickering and Inglis, n.d.

MacArthur, John F., Jr. *Charismatic Chaos.* Grand Rapids: Zondervan, 1992.

MacMillan, John A. *The Authority of the Believer.* Harrisburg, Penn.: Christian Publications, 1980.

McConnell, D. R. *A Different Gospel.* Peabody, Mass.: Hendrickson Publishing, 1988.

McDowell, Josh and Don Stewart. *Handbook of Today's Religions.* San Bernardino, Calif.: Here's Life Publishers, 1983.

————. *Understanding the Cults.* San Bernardino, Calif.: Here's Life Publishers, 1982.

McManus, Una and John Cooper. *Dealing with Destructive Cults.* Grand Rapids: Zondervan, 1984.

Martin, Walter. *The Kingdom of the Cults.* Minneapolis: Bethany House Publishers, 1985.

————. *The New Cults.* Santa Ana, Calif.: Vision House, 1980.

————. *The Rise of the Cults.* Santa Ana, Calif.: Vision House, 1980.

Martz, Larry and Ginny Carroll. *Ministry of Greed.* New York: Weidenfeld and Nicolson, 1988.

Mumford, Bob. *The Problem of Doing Your Own Thing.* Ft. Lauderdale, Fla.: Bob Mumford, 1973.

Murray, Frank S. *The Sublimity of Faith.* Amherst, N.H.: The Kingdom Press, 1981.

Needleman, Jacob and George Baker, eds. *Understanding the New Religions.* New York: Seabury Press, 1978.

Nelson, Shirley. *Fair, Clear and Terrible.* Latham, N.Y.: British American Publishing, 1989.

Ortiz, Juan Carlos. *Disciple.* Carol Stream, Ill.: Creation House, 1975.

Passantino, Robert and Gretchen. *Answers to the Cultist at Your Door*. Eugene, Ore.: Harvest House, 1981.

Paulk, Earl. *Satan Unmasked*. Atlanta: K Dimension, 1984.

Pierson, Arthur T. *George Muller of Bristol*. London: Pickering & Inglis, 1899.

Prince, Derek. *Discipleship, Shepherding, Commitment*. Ft. Lauderdale, Fla.: Derek Prince Publications, 1976.

Rudin, James and Marcia. *Prison or Paradise?* Philadelphia: Fortress Press, 1980.

Sandford, Frank W. *The Golden Light Upon the Two Americas*. Amherst, N.H.: The Kingdom Press, 1974.

Shirer, William L. *A Native's Return*. New York: Simon and Schuster, 1976.

———. *The Nightmare Years*. Boston: Little, Brown, 1984.

Speer, Albert. *Spandau: The Secret Diaries*. New York: MacMillan, 1976.

Stoner, Carroll and Jo Anne Parke. *All God's Children: The Cult Experience—Salvation or Slavery?* New York: Penquin Books, 1979.

Straub, Gerard Thomas. *Salvation for Sale*. Buffalo, N.Y.: Prometheus Books, 1988.

Swindoll, Charles R. *Moral Purity*. Fullerton, Calif.: Insight for Living, 1985.

Thielmann, Bonnie with Dean Merrill. *The Broken God*. Elgin, Ill.: David C. Cook, 1979.

Tozer, A. W. *The Pursuit of God*. Harrisburg, Penn.: Christian Publications, 1948.

Treat, Casey. *Blueprint for Life*. Tulsa, Okla.: Harrison House, 1989.

Trine, Ralph Waldo. *In Tune with the Infinite*. New York: Bobbs-Merrill, 1970.

———. *The Winning of the Best*. Indianapolis: Bobbs-Merrill, n.d.

Underwood, Barbara and Betty Underwood. *Hostage to Heaven: Four Years in the Unification Church by an Ex-Moonie and the Mother Who Fought to Free Her.* New York: Clarkson N. Potter, 1979.

Unger, Merrill F. *The Baptism and Gifts of the Holy Spirit.* Chicago: Moody Press, 1974.

Van Baalen, Jan Karel. *The Chaos of Cults: A Study in Present-Day Isms.* Grand Rapids: Eerdmans, 1962.

Vine, W. E. *An Expository Dictionary of New Testament Words.* London: Oliphants, 1953.

White, Arnold L. *The Almighty and Us.* Ft. Lauderdale, Fla.: n.p., 1979.

Wouk, Herman. *The Caine Mutiny.* Garden City, N.Y.: Doubleday, 1951.